WRITTEN AND SPOKEN

GUIDE TO TITLES

AND FORMS OF ADDRESS

BY

L. G. PINE

B.A.Lond., F.J.I., F.S.A.Scot.,

Editor of *Burke's Peerage, Burke's Landed Gentry, The International Year Book and Stateman's Who Is Who*, etc.

Member International Institute of Genealogy, Corresponding Member, Collegio Araldico, etc., etc.

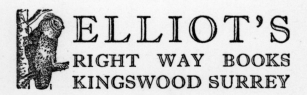

ELLIOT'S
RIGHT WAY BOOKS
KINGSWOOD SURREY

This is a Crown Octavo Book
set in eleven point "Monotype" Times and
produced on Antique Wove paper

Printed in Great Britain by
Wyman and Sons, Ltd., London, Fakenham and Reading

from the use of a title. But although Americans are barred from the use of titles as understood among the older nations of Europe, they certainly have not been backward in inventing all sorts of strange fraternities, elks, shriners, members of phi delta kappa, etc., societies of descendants of noble knights of the Garter, and Kentucky Colonelcies. This sort of thing shows that they are interested in distinctions and that if the ordinary type of honour of Sir or Lord is not available to them, they resort to others which are a somewhat weird imitation of the real thing. Nor can American women be said to lack an interest in titles. In many instances an American lady has become the châtelaine of an ancient home, and borne a title very worthily. Most people will think of Princess Grace of Monaco as an outstanding example of a very graceful American princess.

Then again on the other side of the curtain, almost literally, we have the example of the U.S.S.R. and its satellites. In Russia, the usage is to refer to everyone as comrade, but this has had very little influence on the innate Russian sense of rank and hierarchical distinction. This became particularly apparent during the period of the Second World War and after. Appeal has been made by the Soviet authorities to the sense of distinction and to the feeling of patriotism: Holy Russia made more appeal to the fighting Russians than the austere conceptions of Marxism. Consequently among other relics of the past which were brought back for service were some of the chivalric orders of the Tsars. The Order of St. Alexander Nevsky, which commemorated a great medieval hero, was remodelled, and of course the "Saint" in the title of the Order disappeared, but none the less the Order of Alexander

Nevsky is now in full usage in the U.S.S.R. Moreover, other Tsarist heroes such as the old Marshal Suvorov are commemorated once more by Orders of chivalry which are not conferred lightly but with strict regard to merit and ability. It has been thus found necessary in the Soviet Union to appeal to motives other than the mere economic. There has been a great proliferation of Orders and decorations, not only in Russia but in the other Communist-dominated countries of Europe.

Why do honours so much appeal to the human mind? Surely the true answer lies not only in vanity but in the natural human desire for recognition? This was the reason assigned by the Gloomy Dean, as the late Dr. Ralph Inge was called, for the desire for honours. He felt that most of us are not so selfless that we do not want our work recognized. Now titles are one of the most obvious and inexpensive ways in which this instinct can be gratified. It was Oliver Goldsmith who remarked that the Sovereigns of Europe had found an excellent way to recompense their subjects for the loss of arms, legs, or other injuries by bestowing upon them pretty bits of coloured ribbon.

Whatever the merits of honours, our purpose in this book is to deal first with British honours, and then to pass on to Continental titles. Intrinsically the most difficult system of titles in the world is the British, as will be seen in these pages. In the British system almost every rule which can be laid down has an exception to it. On the other hand, although the European systems of titles are easier in themselves, for reasons which will appear, it is often much more difficult to obtain information about actual titles and their holders than it is in England. The reason for this is that in Europe monarchy flourishes only in a few countries, and even in those where it still exists, honours of an hereditary nature are often not conferred any longer. In Sweden for instance, no patent of nobility has been granted since that which was given to Sven Hedin, the Central Asiatic explorer more than fifty years ago. But wherever a monarchy exists, it is the Fountain of Honour. Britain is the country where the old system of honours is still flourishing in full splendour and it is to Britain that we must first turn and begin with the monarchy.

The Queen—The Fountain of Honour

This means that no honours can be held by British subjects which are not granted by the Queen or which do not flow from her. They must be created by the Crown or recognised by the Crown. It may be as well to clear the latter point first, as it is frequently the subject of much confusion particularly in national newspapers.

The Queen—and Foreign Titles Claimed by British Subjects

It has always been a matter of great concern to the sovereigns of England that their subjects should not accept honours from other sovereigns without seeking their approval first. In the reign of the first Queen Elizabeth, Lord Arundell of Wardour allowed himself to be made a Count of the Holy Roman Empire by the Hapsburg Emperor. On his return home he found himself in trouble with the Queen who objected strongly to his acceptance of the honour. This attitude has persisted and in 1932 a royal warrant was issued by George V in which he laid down the rules regarding certain foreign titles to be borne by British subjects, and then attached a schedule to the warrant giving the names of those who were entitled to foreign titles. This still governs the matter, and disposes in advance of all those cases such as Baron Nugent's where the title does not appear in the schedule. In the case of the ex-Kaiser's grandson, Prince Frederick, the Home Office informed him that he should properly be known as Mr. Mansfield, the name he had adopted on his nationalization as a British subject. The essential feature to grasp is that if a person is under the protection of the British Crown, or comes under that protection by nationalization, he or she must come under the rules laid down from the Crown to govern foreign titles and honours. Now that a number of holders of European titles have become British subjects, it is often hard for the holders not to use their hereditary titles and there is a case for a revision of the warrant mentioned. Consequently, a British subject may not accept or use foreign honours or titles without a licence from the Crown. In the case of an hereditary title this permission will in practice never now be granted. With reference to decorations or other awards of that nature, permission is given subject to various stringent rules set out by the Foreign Office. British military commanders are usually allowed to accept decorations from our allies.

In the case of *foreigners* who become British subjects, they must seek permission to use their inherited titles. They must also have permission to use their foreign coats of arms. Permission for the latter will be given through the Earl Marshal (the Duke of Norfolk) who is head of the College of Arms.

The Origin of Titles

The Queen's own Titles

As Her Majesty is the source of all honour for her subjects her personal titles become of great interest. She is described as Elizabeth the Second, by the Grace of God, of the United Kingdom of Great Britain and Northern Ireland and of her other Realms and Territories, Queen, Head of the Commonwealth, Defender of the Faith.

The use of the term Majesty for our Sovereign dates from the time of Henry VIII (1509–1547). Before him the Sovereigns of England were known as Sovereign Lord Highness. The rest of the Queen's titles are derived from various historical facts. The union of the crowns of England and Scotland brought about a political connection of the two countries in 1603 which has never been severed. Administrative and legislative union did not come until 1707 when the united country became known as Great Britain. The similar union of Great Britain and Ireland in 1801 made the Sovereign ruler of the United Kingdom. With regard to Ireland it was Henry VIII who was first named as King of Ireland. Before his time the English Kings had been Lords of Ireland as they were supposed to hold the country as a fief from the Pope who had given them permission to take it over. In 1541 in an Act of the Irish Parliament, Henry VIII was styled King of Ireland. In 1921 when the south of Ireland became independent of Great Britain, the style of Sovereign of the United Kingdom of Great Britain and Ireland had to be changed to put Northern Ireland in place of Ireland. Similar changes have been necessary since the last war, for the title of Emperor of India, held since 1877, had to be given up when India became independent.

Defender of the Faith

This title has had a curious history. It was bestowed upon Henry VIII by the Pope because Henry had written a defence of the Catholic religion against Martin Luther. When the King broke with Rome over the matter of his marriage to Anne Boleyn, the Pope deprived him of the title. Henry knew what to do and promptly had his Parliament vote him Defender of the Faith (along with his other titles), as his successors have ever since remained.

Head of the Commonwealth

The rest of Her Majesty's titles reflect the enormous empire all over the world (a quarter of the earth's surface) which her father inherited and which has now very largely turned into a commonwealth, in which some of the members, like India, are republics, which acknowledge Her Majesty not as Queen but as Head of the Commonwealth.

Mode of Address to the Queen

In letters this is: "To the Queen's Most Excellent Majesty, or Her Gracious Majesty the Queen." *Letters conclude:* "I remain, with the profoundest veneration, Your Majesty's most faithful and devoted servant." Another form which can be used in writing for the conclusion is: "I have the honour to remain, Madam, Your Majesty's most humble and obedient servant." This form may appeal more in a democratic age.

The *spoken address* is "Your Majesty"—at least that is the style first used when presented to the Queen, but in subsequent speech, "Ma'am" is the usual mode of address with an occasional oblique usage: "Your Majesty will have perceived, etc."

14

"Sir" and "Ma'am" are used in place of Majesty in general spoken usage, as the most simple yet deeply respectful modes of address.

At present we have of course a Queen who is Sovereign in her own right just as her father and grandfather before her, and her husband is therefore her consort. The problem of the Duke of Edinburgh's title long engaged the views of authorities. The Duke of Edinburgh was by birth a Prince of the royal house of Greece, and so of Denmark which is the parent of the Greek Royal line. When he became a British subject, he gave up all rights to the thrones of Greece and of Denmark, and was naturalized as Lieutenant Philip Mountbatten, thus taking the name of his mother's family. When he married Princess Elizabeth he was created a Knight of the Garter (see Chapter 4 on Knights) and Duke of Edinburgh, Earl of Merioneth and Baron Greenwich. He was also given by the late King the style of H.R.H. but he was not correctly styled Prince. This usage of "Prince Philip" did prevail in the popular press mainly because it made a better or more easily set headline than the correct "Duke of Edinburgh". The Duke was given the title of Prince by royal warrant from the Queen in 1957 when his proper style was declared to be: "H.R.H. the Prince Philip, Duke of Edinburgh," etc.

The dropping of the title of Prince by the Duke on his naturalization is a perfect illustration of the usage set out above whereby those who become British subjects cannot use their foreign titles without royal licence.

The Prince of Wales

Since July 1958 we have once more a Prince of Wales.

Written address: "To H.R.H. the Prince of Wales, K.G."
Begin: "Sir."
End: "I have the honour to be, Sir, Your Royal Highness's most humble and obedient servant."

There is no clear precedent for the age at which the Sovereign's son should be made Prince of Wales. The last three Princes of Wales, Edward VII, George V, and Edward VIII were aged respectively one month old, thirty-six years old and sixteen years old. Probably the more usual time for creation was in the early teens, if we follow the medieval precedent. Until the Queen's son was created Prince of Wales, his style was: H.R.H. Prince Charles, Duke of Cornwall, in the Peerage of England, and Duke of Rothesay, Earl of Carrick, and Baron of Renfrew in the Peerage of Scotland, Lord of the Isles and Great Steward of Scotland. These titles belong to Prince Charles because of his mother's accession to the Throne, as they are always borne by the eldest son of the Sovereign. The title of Duke of Cornwall dates from 1337 when Edward III conferred it on his eldest son, Edward the Black Prince. There is also the title of Earl of Chester, but this is conferred with that of Prince of Wales.

The Queen Mother

When Her Majesty succeeded to the Throne, the style of her mother was declared to be Queen Elizabeth the Queen Mother, and not simply Queen Elizabeth, as had been the case with Queen Mary. This new usage avoided the possible confusion which might at times have arisen if "Queen Elizabeth" had been used, alongside the title of Elizabeth II, for the reigning Sovereign.

The full style is: "Her Gracious Majesty Queen Elizabeth the Queen Mother." Letters and spoken address follow the lines set out above for the Queen.

Prince of the Royal Family

Here the usage is (*a*) when the Prince is also a Duke: H.R.H. the Duke of Windsor, or Kent, etc.; (*b*) when the Prince is not a Duke, H.R.H. Prince William (of Gloucester). In formal address in a letter, *begin*: "Sir"; and *conclude*: "I remain with the greatest respect, Sir, Your Royal Highness's most dutiful and obedient servant." The spoken address is "Your Royal Highness", later becoming "Sir".

Princess of the Royal Family

(*a*) For The Princess Royal (the former Princess Mary, daughter of King George V, and now Dowager Countess of Harewood), the written form is: "To H.R.H. the Princess Royal";

(*b*) For Royal Duchesses, such as the Duchess of Gloucester, "To H.R.H. the Duchess of Gloucester";

(*c*) For a Princess who is not a Duchess, for example Princess Margaret, "To H.R.H. the Princess Margaret, etc."

In (*a*), (*b*), and (*c*) begin: "Madam" and *conclude*: "I remain, with the greatest respect, Madam, Your Royal Highness's most dutiful and obedient servant."

The *spoken address* is (at commencement): "Your Royal Highness," thereafter "Ma'am."

With regard to the usage of Prince and Princess for members of the British royal family it should be noted that a great change was made in 1917 by King George V.

He ordained that for the future the children of any Sovereign of the United Kingdom, the children of the sons of any such Sovereign, and the eldest son of the eldest son of the Prince of Wales, shall have and always use the style and title of Royal Highness. The title of Prince or Princess is prefixed to the respective Christian name or is borne with their other titles of honour (such as Duke or other title). At the same time the King ruled that all titles of Royal Highness not borne under the terms of the above, and all titles of Highness or Serene Highness should cease to be borne, except in the cases of those titles already granted and remaining unrevoked. It was also laid down that the grandchildren of the sons of the Sovereign, except the eldest living son of the eldest son of the Prince of Wales, should have the same style as the other sons of Dukes (see Chapter 2, Dukes).

The reason for this ruling was that in 1917 King George V had felt that it would be well to formulate the surname of the royal family. Owing to the great antiquity of the royal pedigree it was not certain what was the royal surname. Surnames came into use fairly late in Europe and consequently a great royal family might well have been established before surnames became general. There was a certain amount of feeling in the 1914–18 war about the fact that the British royal family were of German origin at least in the main line, and that they had many German relatives. Therefore in 1917 King George V issued a proclamation: "Declaring that the name of Windsor is to be borne by His Royal House and Family and Relinquishing the Use of all German Titles and Dignities." This was on 17 July, 1917, and 8 November, 1917, the Titles Deprivation Act became law; this deprived certain persons, such as the Duke of Cumberland, of their British peerages because they were in arms against the British Crown. In addition to the above there were, pursuant upon King George V's wish, a number of changes, in title, so that H.S.H. Prince Louis of Battenberg relinquished all his German titles and became Marquess of Milford Haven, 1917.

Position previous to 1917 for Princes and Princesses

The style of the Princes and Princesses of the Royal House was governed before 1917 by the Letters Patent of Queen Victoria, of 30 January, 1864, whereby the grandsons of the Sovereign in the male line and female line were granted the title of H.R.H. Before this date, 1864, the descendants in the male line were H.H. only, except the sons and daughters of the Sovereign who were H.R.H.

The British Royal Family is connected by marriage and descent with almost all the royal houses of Europe as during the past 300 years there has been a great deal of intermarriage between the royal lines of the different European countries. Most Sovereigns of their respective countries have more in common in blood with other Sovereigns than with the people over whom they reign.

Duke of Lancaster

Occasionally we do hear of instances in which the Sovereign is referred to as Duke of Lancaster. Incidentally this usage is followed whether the reigning Sovereign be King or Queen. When I write "followed" I mean in Lancashire. The late King George VI was addressed as Duke of Lancaster when he was in the county palatine.

This usage dates from the days when John of Gaunt was Duke of Lancaster. He was the fourth son of King Edward III, and it was John of Gaunt's son who became King as Henry IV when Richard II, his cousin, was deposed. The dukedom of Lancaster held by Henry IV then merged in the Crown along with his four earldoms, Hereford, Derby, Lincoln, and Leicester. There are those who say that the Sovereign should not be styled Duke of Lancaster, but to Lancastrians it is a most appropriate title and one which several monarchs, George VI included, have accepted as a graceful act of local homage. There is no reason why loyal Lancastrians should not continue to salute their Sovereign as Duke of Lancaster, and this usage continues for Her present Majesty. It is never Duchess of Lancaster.

Duke of Normandy

There is no reason for this title, as applied to the Sovereign, nor is it ever applied, but I have had queries on the matter. When William the Conqueror conquered England in 1066, he came from Normandy where he was Duke. He held this title from the King of France. William's successor, John, was driven from Normandy in 1204, and by a treaty in 1259 the title of Duke of Normandy was given up by the English Sovereign.

King of France

This former title of the British Sovereign is familiar to most people from the opening pages of the Authorized translation of the Bible, 1611. It dated from the time of Edward III who became King of England in 1327 and later claimed in right of his mother to be King of France.

In 1340 he assumed the title and this usage continued until 1801, despite the fact that the English dominion in France had been terminated in 1453.

King of Hanover

When the last Stuart to reign had died (Queen Anne in 1714), the Elector of Hanover, who was Duke of Brunswick-Luneberg succeeded to the throne of Great Britain and Ireland. Under the Salic Law which prevailed in parts of the continent of Europe, a woman could not reign in Hanover. Consequently when Queen Victoria, the descendant of this Elector (George I), came to the British throne, Hanover passed to her eldest and next uncle, Ernest Augustus, who became therefore Duke of Brunswick-Luneberg, and King of Hanover (the electorate was changed to a kingdom after the Napoleonic Wars, the Holy Roman Empire, to which the Electors used to elect a candidate, having ended in 1806).

It may be of interest to observe that in leaving the presence of a Sovereign it is customary to walk backwards, until out of the room. This is a form of respect, not to turn ones back upon the Sovereign. It is usual to step backwards when leaving the presence of a member of the royal family, and this practice is observed for a few steps at least.

Again, the hat should be removed in the presence of the Sovereign, who will usually graciously request the owner to replace his headgear. No hat which can be classed as part of a uniform is removed, e.g. a jockey brought before the Queen would be correct in remaining covered but should of course stand to attention.

2 | The Nobility

FROM the Fountain of Honour we come to the first persons next in rank to the Crown. It is true that there are people who rank next to the royal family in the order of precedence and who come above the great nobility, but these (such as the two Archbishops, Canterbury and York) do so in right of their offices, and not by title or birth.

In Britain there are two kinds of hereditary title: (i) A peerage. This refers to dukes, marquesses, earls, viscounts and barons; (ii) A baronetcy. This title, although hereditary, does not constitute nobility in the old sense, although the holders of baronetcies are often related to peers, and some 250 baronetcies are held by peers. A special section deals with baronets (see Chapter 3).

The peers are all created by the Sovereign, either by the present Queen or one of her predecessors. Peerages can be created in two ways. The vast majority are created by letters patent which are issued by the Sovereign and which set out the style of the peerage, and how it is to descend. A few old peerages still exist which are relics of the days when they were created by writ of summons. The legal theory is that in the Middle Ages a man was summoned to the House of Lords, to Westminster, and that this created a peerage. If his son were likewise summoned he was the holder of an hereditary peerage. From old peerages of this nature has come the peerage held by a lady in her own right, though a few of the latter class have been created by letters patent in modern days.

The names of the titles held by peers are mostly foreign. Peer itself is a word derived from the French *pair*, meaning equal; its original meaning was that the great feudal lords in France were the peers of the French Crown. It never had this meaning in England but was taken over and adapted to denote a noble. Duke derives from the old Latin *dux*, one of the terms of rank used in the latter stages of the Roman Empire. Marquess derives from *marchio*, one who was responsible for keeping order on a march or frontier. Earl is from Old English *eorl*, itself influenced by the Norse *jarl*. Before the Norman Conquest the title of nobility was *ealdorman* (our modern alderman) but it was displaced by *eorl* (now earl). Viscount is simply from the French, and ultimately from Latin, vice-comes or vice-count. The count was the equivalent of the earl or ruler of a County, and hence our word county, but although an earl's wife is called a countess the count as a term of nobility was never able to drive out the old English earl. Baron is Norman French, meaning the King's Man and was applied after the Norman Conquest to the great landholders who held their lands from the Crown. Baron was in fact a class name, and was applied even to one who was an earl, i.e. the ruler of a county. Most people will remember the *Last of the Barons* by Lord Lytton. The baron of this book title was the Earl of Warwick. But gradually as the other titles of the peerage

—duke, marquess and viscount came along—the title of baron came to denote the lowest grade in the peerage.

Grades of the Peers

In descending order of rank these are: Duke, marquess, earl, viscount and baron. There are five grades within each rank of the peerage. These are, taking dukes as a case, dukes of England, dukes of Scotland, dukes of Great Britain, dukes of Ireland, and dukes of the United Kingdom and dukes of Ireland since the Union (see p. 13). Thus, a duke will rank in order of precedence immediately after the officers of the royal household, but dukes as among themselves will rank in the five classes just shown. These classes have been determined by political arrangements whereby England, Scotland and Ireland came to form the United Kingdom. These arrangements can have some very awkward consequences, for example, few people could understand how Earl Winterton could sit for forty-seven years as an M.P. in the House of Commons, and yet be an earl. Surely a peer could not be a member of the House of Commons? The answer to this conundrum is that under the Union in 1801 of Great Britain and Ireland, only twenty-eight Irish peers could be elected (by the remaining Irish peers) to sit in the House of Lords. The other Irish peers were free to offer themselves as candidates for the House of Commons. Thus it came about that a "pukka" earl, Lord Winterton, was Father of the House of Commons. To make matters a little more complicated, when Earl Winterton retired from the Commons, he would not have been able to sit in the Lords unless he had been given a peerage of the United Kingdom which always carries with it the right to a seat in the Lords. So he was

created Baron Turnour, in the peerage of the United
Kingdom, and proceeded to take his seat in the House of
Lords in a rank two degrees lower in the peerage than the
earldom which he had inherited.

In the Roll of the Lords Spiritual and Temporal which
is issued by Her Majesty's Stationery Office, and which
gives the names of those peers who are entitled to sit in
the Upper House, there is a short appendix which lists
seventy-seven peers who are peers of Scotland or of
Ireland, but who are shown on the Roll as peers of the
United Kingdom, because they hold a United Kingdom
peerage as well as the Scottish or Irish titles. The Roll
adds that these peers are usually addressed by the titles
of their higher rank, when they are in the House of
Lords.

The position of Scottish peers is really much less
advantageous than that of the Irish peers. Under the
Treaty of Union between England and Scotland in 1707,
sixteen Scottish peers were to be elected by their fellows
to serve in the House of Lords for the life of each Parliament. The Scottish peers who were not elected were
not, and are not eligible for membership of the House of
Commons. A peer cannot vote in elections of the House
of Commons, and so it comes about that a Scottish peer
who does not possess a United Kingdom peerage and who
is not a representative peer for Scotland, is completely
unenfranchised. As Lord Belhaven has recently pointed
out in his own case, his property can be the subject of
government action by taxation and death duties and yet
he has no say whatever in legislation. Furthermore the
Scottish peerage has dwindled since 1707 because no other
Scottish peerages have been created since then, whereas

the Irish peerage is much larger than the Scottish peerage because under the terms of the Treaty of Union between Great Britain and Ireland, Irish peerages were created right into the present century.

This is a book dealing with titles, and not with peerage law, but at the end of this chapter an account is given of such matters as titles which are called out of abeyance, life peerages, etc. The Spiritual Lords—Archbishops and Bishops—are dealt with separately in a chapter on Ecclesiastical titles.

Duke, Mode of Address

In letters: "To His Grace the Duke of ——."

Begin: "My Lord Duke." *Conclude:* "I have the honour to be (or I remain), my Lord Duke, Your Grace's most humble and obedient servant."

Spoken address is "Your Grace".

The above styles do not apply to royal dukes, whose styles are set out in Chapter 1.

Duchess, Mode of Address

Letters: "To Her Grace the Duchess of ——."

Begin: "Madam." *Conclude:* "I have the honour to be, Madam, Your Grace's most humble and obedient servant."

Spoken address: "Your Grace."

Marquess, Mode of Address

Letters: "To the Most Hon. the Marquess of ——."

Begin: "My Lord Marquess." *Conclude:* "I have the honour to be, My Lord Marquess, etc."

Spoken address: "My Lord" or "Your Lordship."

Earl, Mode of Address

Letters: "To the Rt. Hon. the Earl of ——."

Begin: "My Lord." *Conclude:* "I have the honour to be, my Lord, Your Lordship's obedient and humble servant."

Spoken address: "My Lord" or "Your Lordship."

Viscount, Mode of Address

Letters: "To the Rt. Hon. the Viscount ——." Otherwise as for an Earl.

Baron, Mode of Address

Letters: "To the Rt. Hon. Lord ——." Otherwise as for an Earl.

Marchioness

Letters: "To the Most Hon. the Marchioness of ——."

Begin: "Madam." *Conclude:* "I have the honour to be, Madam, Your Ladyship's obedient and humble servant.

Spoken address: "My Lady" or "Your Ladyship."

Countess (Earl's Wife), Viscountess, and Baroness

Letters: "To the Right Hon. the Countess of ——." "To the Rt. Hon. the Viscountess ——." "To the Rt. Hon. Lady ——."

Otherwise the forms are the same as for a Marchioness.

Difference between formal and informal Modes of Address

The styles set out above are extremely formal and are rarely used nowadays unless by servants seeking a reference or by tradespeople who are very anxious to obtain an order. In the case of *Burke's Peerage* where some 35,000 proofs have to be sent out, the form normally used on the questionnaires is "Sir or Madam", and ending with "Yours Faithfully". This form is used for peers, peeresses and for all others. It is also used in speech. Rarely during my experience at *Burke's* has the formal style set out above been used, except in the case of dukes. Usually when I have to write to a peer, I write "Sir", and conclude "I am, Sir, yours faithfully". This gives an air of formality to the letter while avoiding the abject style, "Your creeping, humble and obsequious slave, etc.".

In the case of all the four ranks of the peerage, apart from the dukes, that is, marquess, earl, viscount and baron, the normal mode of reference is "Lord X", whether the peer in question is an earl or a baron. Instances abound in writing of references to Lord Cholmondeley, Lord Birkenhead, Lord Scarsdale, and Lord Beaverbrook, etc., where these four peers are respectively Marquess, Earl, Viscount and Baron.

The same applies to their ladies, who are termed Lady X, whether they are marchionesses, countesses, baronesses, or viscountesses. Ladies whose husbands are baronets or knights are also styled Lady ——.

Titles of Children of Peers

I have purposely left these to the present place because some words of explanation are necessary. In Britain, unlike other European lands, the children of the nobility do not form a legal caste. Any titles which they bear are purely of courtesy. These titles have become prescribed by centuries of usage but otherwise have no power. They do not resemble the titles of peers which are laid down in their letters of creation (letters patent) but are the result of generations of growth. Anyone who refused to use these courtesy titles would certainly be very boorish, but on the other hand the victim of his rudeness would have no formal redress. Fashions in modes of address for the eldest sons of peers have varied much, for example the Hon. Charles Stuart, commonly called Lord Linton, is a style which appeared on a document over 100 years ago.

With this premise I will now set out the styles used for the children of peers. In the case of dukes, marquesses and earls, the eldest son takes the father's second title, as a courtesy usage. Why does the duke, marquess or earl have a secondary title? Being high in the ranks of the peerage, he is assumed to hold the lower ranks also, and thus on the creation of a commoner as an earl (instead of the advancement of a peer, who is a baron or viscount, to an earldom), there is usually conferred upon him a viscounty also. Thus Earl Jowitt when so created in 1951 received also the Viscounty of Stevenage as well as the Earldom of Jowitt. (It is true that at the time Earl Jowitt was already a peer as Baron Jowitt and Viscount Jowitt.) A more apposite example is that of Mr. Attlee who in 1955 was created Earl Attlee and Viscount Prestwood of Walthamstow. The latter title is that borne by his only son.

Duke's Son

A duke's eldest son therefore takes by courtesy his father's second title and is addressed personally as if he were a peer. The eldest son of an eldest son takes by courtesy the third title of his grandfather. (In the case of a duke it is most improbable that he will not also have other peerage honours beside his dukedom, and so there will be plenty of titles for the son and grandson. Should a commoner be created a duke, he will receive other titles in addition to his dukedom. Thus, Lieutenant Philip Mountbatten was created Duke of Edinburgh, Earl of Merioneth and Baron Greenwich. (The reference to a commoner here is of course a technicality, as the Prince had relinquished his former royal status previous to his engagement to Princess Elizabeth, see p. 15.) When Prince Henry, third son of George V, was created Duke of Gloucester he also received the titles of Earl of Ulster and Baron Culloden. In the case of a royal creation it will be observed that all three parts of the United Kingdom are represented in the titles. The Duke's eldest son and the latter's eldest son are addressed just as if they were really peers, but as they are not peers they are not styled, Rt. Hon. The duke's younger sons are addressed by the title Lord prefixed to their Christian names, thus Lord Randolph Churchill (father of Sir Winston Churchill). Their letters are addressed: "To Lord John——." *Begin:* "My Lord." *Conclude:* "I have the honour to be, my Lord, Your Lordship's most obedient and humble servant."

Spoken address: "My Lord" or "Your Lordship." The wife of one of these younger sons takes the title of Lady and is addressed as "Lady (John) ——."

NOTE.—As the eldest son and eldest son's son of a duke are treated as peers their wives will be treated as peeresses and will therefore be dealt with as regards styles under the rank as given in the categories above.

Duke's Daughter

She is addressed and styled as Lady Mary ——, followed by her surname as in the case of her brothers, the younger sons.

Letters begin: "Madam." *Conclude:* "I have the honour to be, Madam, Your Ladyship's most obedient and humble servant."

Spoken address: "My Lady" or "Your Ladyship."

If she is married to a man who is not a peer, she still retains her title and only her surname is changed. But if she is married to a peer, the courtesy title which she bore as a duke's daughter is lost in the higher rank.

The usage of Lady Mary Smith for the daughter of a duke (and the same usage applies to a daughter of a marquess or an earl) is often confused in newspapers and uninformed writing. Lady Mary Smith who is mentioned in a newspaper report may well be not the daughter of duke, marquess or earl but the wife of a knight. The use of Mary between her title and surname is due occasionally to ignorance but often to a mistaken attempt to avoid confusion when there are more than one of the same surname among titled ladies. The correct way to deal with this very real problem for all who have to write on the subject of titled people is to put "Lady (Mary) Smith". The use of the parentheses makes it quite clear that the Christian name is not to be used as a title, and that it is printed solely for purposes of differentiation.

The customary right of a duke's daughter to retain her style of address when she marries a man who is her inferior in rank or at least not a peer, leads to the situation whereby we read of Mr. Anthony and Lady Mary Jones.

31

Marquess's Sons

Addressed in the same way as those of a duke, the eldest son taking his father's second title.

Marquess's Daughters

Addressed in the same way as a duke's daughters.

Earl's Sons

The eldest son takes his father's second title and is addressed personally as if he were a peer, his rank being for this purpose that of Viscount or Baron. The eldest son of an eldest son is addressed as if his father were a peer, i.e. as the Hon.

The younger sons of an earl and their wives are addressed in the same way as those of a baron, see below.

Viscount's Sons

They and their wives, also the daughters of a viscount are addressed in the same way as for those of a baron.

Baron's Sons

They have the style of Hon. before their names and it is of course in this case incorrect to address them in writing as Mr. or Esquire.

Letters: "To the Hon. (John) ——."

Begin: "Sir." *Conclude:* "I have the honour to be, Sir, Your obedient servant." *Spoken address:* "Sir." Wives of barons' sons are addressed as the Hon. Mrs. (John) ——, unless they are of higher rank than a viscount's daughter. In other words if an Hon. has married the daughter of an earl, marquess or duke, her style will be that of the Hon. Lady Mary ——.

Baron's Daughters

They have the style of Hon. prefixed before their Christian names. *Letters:* "To the Hon. Mary ——."

If she is married the change is in her surname. If she is married to a commoner she is styled: "The Hon. Mrs. John ——." If married to a knight or baronet: "The Hon. Lady ——." If married to a peer, she no longer uses the prefix Hon., because the rank of her husband is higher than hers before her marriage.

Letters begin: "Madam." *Conclude:* according to the rank of the husband. *Spoken address:* "Madam" (or according to the rank of the husband).

Widow of a Peer

The styles used for the widow of a peer illustrate in a very excellent manner the change which can take place in customs of address. Until about twenty years ago the normal usage was to refer to the widow of a peer as the Dowager Lady ——, or Dowager Countess of —— or whatever her rank might be. The term dowager means a widow who is in possession of a dower or jointure. The term as used for ladies in the peerage served to distinguish the holder from the wife of her husband's heir. Consequently the term dowager was not used until the arrival of a wife for the heir to the title. Until that time the widow of a peer was and is known simply as Lady X.

The word dowager is now very seldom used. For the period of roughly the past twenty years many if not most widows of peers have preferred to style themselves thus:

Mary, Countess Howe, etc. This is a great change from the style of Dowager Countess Howe, etc., but it has one great advantage because it does differentiate between two dowagers. It sometimes happens that there are two widows of peers in the same family while the reigning peer is married. To distinguish between his mother and grandmother the use of the Christian names before their titles is extremely serviceable.

For the general question of women's titles see Chapter 6.

It may be added that a widow of a peer who marries again loses her title and takes the style of her new husband if he is a commoner or whatever his rank. Similarly with women who are divorced; they retain their former husband's rank while they are unmarried, but lose it and take the new husband's on second marriage. This matter is dealt with at greater length in the chapter referred to above.

Life Peerages

This subject is now very much in the public eye owing to the act passed by the Government in 1958 whereby the Crown is empowered to create life peerages which can be conferred on men and on women. Fourteen such life peerages were created in July 1958, four of them being granted to women. Life peerages are not new. They have been conferred over several centuries and the opinion of some of the greatest lawyers has been that the Sovereign has the power to create them. Unfortunately in the seventeenth and eighteenth centuries the members of the House of Lords took a great dislike to life peerages which they considered somewhat beneath their dignity. They raised strong objections to them, with the result that a long period elapsed in which few if any life peerages were made. Then in 1856 Lord Wensleydale was created a life peer, but the House of Lords refused to allow him to take his seat. After twenty years of wrangling it was agreed under the Appellate Jurisdiction Acts from 1876 that life peerages could be created on behalf of some of the judges in order that they should be able to sit in the House of Lords during its activities as a Court of Law. This concession was strictly limited and there were never more than about twelve or thirteen life peers (all eminent lawyers) in the House of Lords.

A life peerage is just as much nobility as an hereditary peerage and the styles of life peers do not differ from those of the hereditary peers.

Peerages held by Women

No woman had ever sat as a peeress in the House of Lords until the creations under the Life Peerages Act, 1958, but several other women hold peerages apart from the recently created life peeresses. These are known as peeresses in their own right. They are women who have inherited peerages from their fathers or who have received a peerage because their husbands did not live long enough to receive the honour. There are twenty-five women who thus hold peerage honours. They are addressed as other titled women who hold their titles in right of their husbands. But a complication arises when these peeresses marry. Thus one of the greatest ladies in Scotland is the Countess of Erroll. She is married to Captain Sir Iain Moncreiffe, Bt. She is known however as the Countess of Erroll, and never as Lady Moncreiffe (except as indicated overleaf for reference purposes).

The other twenty-four ladies are usually referred to as, for example, the Countess of Seafield (Mrs. Studley-Herbert), where the title which they bear is followed by their married name.

Peerages held in abeyance or dormant

A peerage can become dormant because the heir to it is not known, or it can fall into abeyance because there is no single heir. These cases hardly affect use of title but they can be mentioned here because there are people who style themselves by some title to which they have not yet proved their claim. Such people are to be sharply distinguished from those who are merely impostors but they ought not to use a title until they have proved their right to it. The proper way to set about this is to apply to the Home Secretary who will notify the applicant of what is required of him. It should be added that the claiming of a title is an expensive business, involving the expenditure of perhaps some thousands of pounds.

Titled Persons who do not use their Titles

From time to time instances occur in which someone who has succeeded to a peerage or a baronetcy does not wish to use the title. In one case a baronet who had newly inherited his title wrote to me that he did not wish to be addressed as Sir —— but would continue to be addressed as Mr. ——.

In cases such as these where the wishes of the individual are known they should be respected. Many amusing instances do, however, occur through people not wishing to use their proper titles. When Sidney Webb was created Lord Passfield his wife refused to use the title and so they were introduced at parties as Lord Passfield and Mrs. Sidney Webb. Both Lord Passfield and his wife are now dead. An hereditary title cannot be renounced in the sense that a man can refuse to accept it. Willy-nilly he has to become the tenth baron or ninth baronet as the case may be. He cannot—to use the language of the House of Lords in 1678—extinguish an hereditary honour created by the Crown. But equally he cannot be compelled to use it.

Scottish and Irish Peers

Something has been said above about Scottish and Irish peers whose titles do not carry with them the right to a seat in the House of Lords. It is only necessary to add that the accident—arising from historical circumstances— that they do not sit in the Lords does not of course affect their nobility or peerage, or the manner in which they are addressed.

The style of Rt. Hon. used for all peers below the rank of marquess has been challenged in recent times. It has been argued that earls, viscounts and barons should be addressed simply as the Earl of ——, etc., without the style of Rt. Hon. This controversy was eventually settled by a ruling from the College of Arms. In fact the controversy should never have begun.

The usage of Rt. Hon. before the names of earls, viscounts and barons was a custom which began in the days when most if not all members of the Privy Council were peers. Privy Councillors were addressed as the Rt. Hon. and from this the usage spread so that all peers even those who were not Privy Councillors were addressed in the same manner. It was thus an excellent example of the way in which a social usage and a courteous one grew up by habit. No one thought of challenging it until an attempt was made a few years ago to differentiate between peers who were members of the Privy Council and those who were not. The former who are now in a small minority were to retain the appellation of Rt. Hon., the latter were to be addressed as simply Lord X or Y. Fortunately this strange idea was soon overthrown and the prevalent style of Rt. Hon. for all peers below the rank of marquess was confirmed.

3 | The Order of Baronets

I̶T IS much easier to say how a baronet should be addressed than to describe what he is, and so we begin in this chapter by giving the styles of a baronet before the explanation of his rank and its origin.

Written address: Letters begin: "To Sir John Smith, Baronet."

Begin: "Sir." *Conclude:* "I have the honour to be, Sir, Your obedient servant."

NOTE.—Above, the word Baronet is given in full, but the correct form is, according to the Standing Council of the Baronetage (for which see below), "Bt." The abbreviation used in general is "Bart." Few people write Baronet in full; the normally used form Bart. has the great advantage that it can be used in speech, that is pronounced, whereas Bt. simply cannot be pronounced. The Standing Council just mentioned is not an official body.

Spoken address: "Sir", Sir George ——."

Wives of Baronets are addressed as, for example Lady Smith (unless they have higher ranks in their own families), so that an earl's daughter would be Lady Mary Smith.

Letters to Baronets' Wives *begin:* "Madam." *Conclude:* "I have the honour to be, Madam, Your Ladyship's obedient servant."

Spoken address: "My Lady" or "Your Ladyship." The same proviso mentioned for peeresses applies here since (see p. 27) no one of good social or educational status would address anyone as "My Lady".

Widow of a Baronet

As in the case of a peer's widow: "Emma, Lady Smith" or "The Dowager Lady Smith."

Baronet's Children

The children are addressed as simply "Esquire" or "Miss".

It should be noted that if the son of a viscount or a baron or the younger son of an earl is created a baronet, his style is the Hon. Sir James Smith, Bt., and his wife is the Hon. Lady Smith.

Banneret and Baronet

In many old documents there are references to bannerets. As the name may be confused with baronet it may be as well to distinguish between them. A banneret or more amply a knight banneret is described as a knight who was entitled to lead a company of vassals under his banner. The banner differed from the pennon of the knight. The pennon was the forked swallow-tail flag familiar to most people who have seen medieval pictures. The banner was squarely cut and it is alleged that in the Middle Ages the especially brave knight was rewarded for his gallantry by having his pennon cut so as to take off the forked ends and leave the banneret or diminutive of the banner. His degree of knight banneret then gave him precedence over other knights but not over barons.

Thus banneret was a title borne and conferred for deeds done on the battlefield. It is said that it existed in Switzerland and in Italy in the Middle Ages. Some authorities in England contend that the titles banneret and baronet are the same. Thirteen instances of the use of the word baronet have been found between the reign of Edward II (1307–1327) and that of Elizabeth I (1558–1603). In one of these instances, in 1340, one William de la Pole received from King Edward III the dignity of a baronet, this title to be for himself and his heirs.

Origin of the Order of Baronets

James I (1603–1625) like his later Stuart successors was always in need of ready money. He could raise only limited sums for regular use from his Parliaments. He therefore had recourse to sales of honours and in fact he was the first person to introduce the sale of titles and dignities into England. Anyone who was knighted by him was fairly sure of having to pay for the honour, while anyone who declined a knighthood was certain to have to pay a fine. Thus the Crown obtained revenue from the sale or the refusal of honours.

It is supposed that it was the researches of Sir Robert Cotton, an eminent scholar of the early seventeenth century which set King James upon the plan of creating a new hereditary order. Cotton turned up some cases such as that of William de la Pole in which the hereditary title of baronet had been conferred, and this may well have suggested to James I that he could turn the title to good account. He did so, and in 1611 the King set forth in a royal decree the intention of creating a degree of nobility between Barons and Knights. The idea was that in medieval times there had been greater and lesser barons. The greater barons had gradually come to fill the House of Lords, whereas the lesser barons had tended to become country squires.

In Scotland the distinction between the greater and the lesser barons did not lose its force. Even now there is a distinction between a lord of parliament (in other words a peer) and a lord who is not of parliament. The latter is usually called in Scotland a laird, and he often holds a small barony as part of his title. This is a feudal survival peculiar to Scotland.

King James went on to state that none would be admitted to the dignity of baronet who did not have a certain revenue of £1,000 per annum or the equivalent in rents from lands. Also the would-be baronet must be a gentleman in the sense that he must have arms from his grandfather on his father's side. The order was to be restricted to 200. A further requirement was that each new baronet should agree to give a total of £1,095—this being sufficient to keep thirty foot soldiers at the rate of 8*d*. per day for three years, these men to be employed for service in Ireland. The baronets to this day bear the famous Red Hand of Ulster (the badge of Ulster) on their coats of arms, and thus the settlement of Ulster in the early seventeenth century is connected with the order of baronets. The cost of passing the letters patent was about £1,200 over and above the expenses already mentioned. Despite James I's promise not to create more than 200 baronets, 223 were actually created during his reign. His son, Charles I, formed a plan for the settlement of Nova Scotia. To effect this the King created an order of baronets of Scotland. The number of these was not to exceed 150 and much the same conditions were to prevail as with the baronets of England. These Nova Scotia baronets were to have large legislative and commercial rights in Nova Scotia. During Charles I's reign 253 baronets of England were created, 21 baronets of Ireland and 103 of Scotland—a total of 377, and to this possibly another 15 could be added, whose patents were made out during the Civil War. The badge of the Scottish baronets was a saltire (like a St. Andrew's cross) with a small escutcheon on the saltire on which were shown the arms of Scotland, and the escutcheon had an imperial crown above it.

The total number of baronets at present exceeds 1,500, of whom about 250 are peers also. Thus the intentions of the original founders have long since been surpassed; indeed it is clear from their record during the earliest days of the institution that little regard was had to the idea of maintaining the order at 200 or 150.

The different classes of baronet may be given as follows:

Baronets of England, 1611.

Baronets of Ireland, 1611.

Baronets of Scotland, 1625.

Baronets of Great Britain, 1707.

Baronets of the United Kingdom, 1801.

By a royal warrant of King George V (May 10th, 1929), all baronets, other than those of Scotland, may wear round their necks a badge which shows the arms of Ulster (the bloody hand surmounted by an Imperial crown), and suspended from an orange tawny ribbon. Baronets of Scotland have the badge described above, showing the arms of Scotland, and suspended from a ribbon of orange tawny.

The order of baronets has had a chequered history, largely due to the inexact manner in which the founder, James I, set it up. From the very beginning there have been great arguments and disputes over the precedence of the order. At present it ranks a long way behind the lowest degree in the peerage, that of baron. Baronets in fact rank behind Knights of the Garter, of the Thistle and of Patrick, and after barons' younger sons, and sons of Lords of Appeal in Ordinary.

Nearly 300 years after the foundation of the order, an association was made, which was known at first as The Honourable Society of the Baronetage. This was formed in 1898 but was afterwards dissolved and recreated under the title of The Standing Council of the Baronetage in 1902. Under this title it still exists and its object is to guard the privileges and status of the baronets and to protect their interests.

The members must be baronets or their wives or widows, and also associate members who are the heirs to baronetcies or the children of lawful baronets. This Standing Council achieved one of its great objects when it secured the preparation and maintenance of a Roll of Baronets at the Home Office. On 8 February, 1910, a royal warrant was issued by King Edward VII which prescribed that an Official Roll of Baronets should be prepared and kept in the Home Office. No person whose name is not entered on this Roll can be received as a baronet or be addressed or mentioned by that title in any civil or military commission, letters patent or other official document. From time to time I have been consulted by persons who think that they are entitled to be baronets by inheritance but who do not want to go to the expense and trouble of registering their succession with the Home Office. I have always pointed out to them that while no crime is committed in calling oneself Sir or Baronet, no official recognition can be given to a baronetcy title unless it is recorded on the Home Office Roll. One of the consequences of this is that the eldest son of a baronet who would unquestionably succeed him in title as much as in estate will not be styled Sir on an official document unless he has troubled to record his succession with the Registrar of the Baronetage at the Home Office. This means that for example in an invitation to Buckingham Palace to a luncheon or garden party he and his wife are liable to be addressed as Mr. and Mrs. —— instead of as Sir John and Lady ——.

As a result of the efforts of the Standing Council other improvements in the position of the baronets have been made. They were not represented at the coronation of George IV, William IV or of Queen Victoria, but they were represented at the coronation of Edward VII and of subsequent Sovereigns. Badges of their rank may now be worn by baronets as indicated above.

One of the most interesting former privileges of the baronets was that of having their eldest sons knighted on the latter attaining the age of twenty-one. This was definitely laid down in the patents whereby a baronetcy was created, and many such knighthoods were conferred, without the normal expenses formerly associated with a knighthood. This privilege gradually fell into disuse, however, and after 1827 (in the reign of George IV) it was decreed by the Crown that for the future no letters patent issued for a baronetcy should contain the clause which allowed for the knighting of the baronet's eldest son at twenty-one. It was expressly mentioned, however, that this new ruling was without prejudice to the rights under former patents, so that the numerous baronetcies which existed before 1827 and which still exist have still this privilege. It is never claimed now.

There is an interesting difference between a baronet, a peer and a knight in respect to the style by which they may be addressed after their having been created baronet, knight or peer in the New Year's or Birthday Honours List.

People often want to know how to address a message of congratulation to a new peer or knight. In both cases the mode of address remains what it was before the new dignity was conferred until in the case of (i) a peer, his title has been gazetted and (ii) a knight, until he has received the accolade. In the matter of peerage we obviously cannot address Mr. Rank as Lord Rank until we know whether he will choose the title of Rank or use some other name, for example Mr. Lyttelton became Viscount Chandos. His peerage must therefore be gazetted in the *London Gazette* before we can use the proper style. A knight is not a knight until his shoulder has been tapped with the Sovereign's sword, and he has been told to "rise, Sir Herbert". Not long ago a case occurred in which the recipient of a peerage died before the list was published (Dr. Garbett, Archibishop of York). He was never a peer, but had he lived after the list had been published and then died, we should not have known how to denominate him because the title would not have been gazetted.

In the case of baronets the matter is quite different. As soon as a baronetcy is mentioned as being conferred in the Honours Lists, the new baronet may be addressed as

Sir John Smith. The reason for this is that a baronetcy unlike a knighthood does not call for the accolade. Again, although it will be gazetted in due course, the title cannot be different from the style of the man's name at the time of creation. The new baronet may elect to be styled Sir John Smith of Purley in the county of Surrey, but Sir John he must be.

There is no restriction on a baronet from changing his surname. This must seem very curious if we regard, as we ought to do, the order of baronets as the sixth degree of nobility. If Sir John Smith wishes to be known as Sir John Beswetherick, there is nothing to prevent him from doing so. On the other hand it would be quite impossible for a peer, for example, Lord Beaverbrook, to decide that in future he would be known as Lord New Brunswick. His patent forbids such a change. Yet a baronet can do this and get away with it. An interesting example is that of the Scottish baronetcy of Dalyell of the Binns, which was created in 1685. The patent of this baronetcy allows it to descend to heirs general as well as heirs male, and thus it has passed through several lines, which have assumed the name of Dalyell. The third baronet was the nephew of the second, and was first known as Sir James Menteith, afterwards being described as Sir James Dalyell, 3rd Baronet. The last holder of the baronetcy was Sir James Bruce Dalyell, 9th Baronet. His paternal name was Cornwall. He left an only child, a daughter who became Mrs. Loch. Her husband assumed the name of Dalyell and their son Thomas is the heir to the baronetcy. Thus this family has really ceased some generations back to be Dalyells, in the male line, and on one occasion at least has used the surname other than Dalyell for a time.

There is incidentally on record the case of a lady who was made a baronetess. She was a Mrs. Thomas Jopson, who later married Thomas Bolles. She was created a Baronetess of Scotland with remainder to heirs male and assignees. She was designated as Lady Mary Bolles, Baronetess. Her successor was her grandson, William Jopson, who became Sir William Jopson, another instance of change of name in a baronet.

The order of baronets despite its misfortunes has some very fine advantages over the peerage. The peers have frequently been under fire, and not only in modern times, from the enemies of privilege and hereditary position. In the times of the Civil War in England, in the reign of Charles I, the House of Lords was abolished, and on the grounds that long and painful experience had shown them to be enemies of the people of England. The peers from their eminent position in the Upper House are the objects of attack by all sorts of persons. Their presence in the legislature is much objected against by friends of democracy so-called. But a baronet does not suffer from this disability. He does not have the right to a seat in the House of Lords, and on the other hand he is not debarred from sitting in the House of Commons if he can get himself elected to the House.

Thus a baronet has the best of both worlds, an hereditary title, which carries with it no legislative rights or position and yet the potentiality of membership in the House of Commons.

Perhaps it is this duality which has led Socialists in recent years to object to baronetcies. They cannot bear the thought that a man may enjoy anything except alleged social service, or a dumb and miserable equality. Consequently during the six years of Socialist rule from 1945–51, only eight baronetcies were conferred, and these mostly on retiring Lord Mayors of London. The Lord Mayor of London by custom extending back some two centuries is made a knight on taking office and a baronet on laying it down. The Socialists did not feel able to break this tradition but they restricted the creation of baronetcies almost to this.

On the return of Sir Winston's government in 1951 the creation of baronetcies was resumed.

4 | Knights

A DISTINCTION has to be made at once between Knights Bachelor and Knights of Orders of Chivalry like the Garter. As a great deal of confusion exists on the subject of Knights Bachelor it is just as well to try to clear this up at the outset.

Knights Bachelor

It is thought, for example by Dr. W. A. Shaw in his *Knights of England*, p. xli, that the word bachelor as applied to knights was derived from a confusion between the Norman French word *battalere* or *battalier* (meaning fighting tenants) and the low Latin word *baccalaurii*. The latter became rendered into English as bachelor. The Bachelor of Arts was a person who had attained a position of honour and distinction as the holder of the first degree, the Master being greater and the Dr. greatest. Similarly with knighthood the Knight Bachelor was the first position in chivalry. Whatever the historical explanation there can be no doubt that a Knight Bachelor represents the original basic order of chivalry from which all the later orders such as the Garter, the Bath, St. Michael and St. George are developments. The original order of chivalry came into existence during the Middle Ages and from the feudal

50

system. We have great difficulty in tracing this development because little if any direct evidence exists, and also a cloud of legend has distracted the attention of later historians. Thus even as late as 300 years ago writers of books on chivalric orders would actually refer to the Order of the Knights of the Round Table. Knighthood in any particle of the true historic sense did not exist in the days when the real King Arthur lived, namely in the sixth century when the Roman Empire in Britain had crashed and the Saxons were invading the country. Knighthood as we understand it evolved slowly from the times of the tenth century and was an integral part of feudal society and of warfare until the decline of the Middle Ages led to the disappearance of mailed chivalry from the battlefield.

The use of the title Sir as applied to a knight came gradually and may be said to date from the thirteenth century.

Mode of Address

This is the same as for a baronet, thus: "To Sir John Smith." The name should be followed by the abbreviation, Knt. or Kt., or if very formal, Kt. Bach. *Letters begin:* "Sir." *Conclude:* "I have the honour to be, Sir, your obedient servant." *Spoken address:* is "Sir". Wives of Knights are addressed as "Lady Smith" (unless they have higher rank from their own families). *Letters begin:* "Madam." *Conclude:* "I have the honour to be, Madam, your Ladyship's obedient servant." Formal *spoken address:* "My Lady" or "Your Ladyship" (but see pp. 27 and 28). The children of knights are not entitled to any other title than Mr., Esq., or Miss.

It is quite easy to dispose of all the knights in the few

lines above, regarding their mode of address. The only additional item is that in the case of an order of chivalry, the appropriate letters are given after the name, thus K.G. for Knight of the Garter, K.C.B. for Knight Commander of the Order of the Bath.

The Knights Bachelor as already pointed out really represent the true and original knights, the famous knights in armour whose rare chivalry and more usual cruelty and bestiality fill the pages of medieval history. As time passed the sovereigns of Europe felt inclined to create other orders which would give recognition to special merit. It was a long time before these special orders such as the Garter took away from the general merit of the ordinary order of knighthood but as armour passed out of use and the knight-errant ceased to be a figure of use in war, the greater orders took on more splendour and the degree of knighthood now known as that of Knight Bachelor began to be looked on as reserved for those who possessed only ordinary merits.

Today whenever a title is to be conferred on someone for whom one of the greater orders is not applicable, he is made a Knight Bachelor. Each of the orders has its own peculiar abbreviations, several of them have classes, some of which do not carry titles at all before the recipient's name. A full list of the British Orders of Knighthood is as follows: :

Order of the Garter.
Order of the Thistle.
Order of St. Patrick.
Order of the Bath.
Order of Merit.
Order of the Star of India.

Order of St. Michael and St. George.
Order of the Indian Empire.
Royal Victorian Order.
Order of the British Empire.
Orders of the Companions of Honour.
Distinguished Service Order.
Imperial Service Order.

Of these, four—the Order of Merit, the Companions of Honour, the Distinguished Service Order and the Imperial Service Order—do not carry a title (nor are there classes in them) but their recipients can use the distinguishing appreviations after their names. Thus O.M., C.H., D.S.O., and I.S.O. The Garter, Thistle and St. Patrick do not have any classes but one. The number of knights is limited. The distinguishing abbreviations, which are used after the name are: K.G., K.T., K.P. The Order of St. Patrick is not now conferred in deference to an Irish republican sentiment which it does nothing to appease.

The Most Honourable Order of the Bath has three classes. The first is G.C.B., i.e. Knight Grand Cross, an extra special distinction within the Order. The second is K.B. or K.C.B., which is the more usual modern abbreviation, Knight Commander of the Bath. The third is C.B. which is Companion of the Order of the Bath. The Companion in this as in other orders is untitled but has the distinguishing letters after his name. Incidentally the Order of the Bath does really have to do with a bath in its origins, because the persons to be made knights were wont to take a bath previous to receiving the accolade. It was the custom to make a number of knights before a coronation and these were specifically referred to as Knights of the

Bath. The custom of creating Knights of the Bath in this particular manner ceased with the coronation of Charles II.

The Most Exalted Order of the Star of India

There are three classes: Knights Grand Commanders. They are shown as G.C.S.I., having these letters after their names. Knights Commanders: K.C.S.I., and Companions: C.S.I.

This Order was instituted in 1861, and was used to reward the services of eminent persons, such as the Princes and Chiefs of India, but has fallen into disuse since the British gave self rule to India in 1947.

The Most Distinguished Order of St. Michael and St. George

Instituted in 1818 to reward British subjects who serve in British overseas possessions or who render services in connection with the Empire. There are three classes: Knights Grand Cross, Knights Commanders and Companions. They are denominated by the letters G.C.M.G., K.C.M.G., and C.M.G. respectively.

Grand Cross

It may be remarked at this stage that a Knight Grand Cross is addressed as Sir in exactly the same manner as a Knight, or Knight Companion, but has the letters such as G.C.M.G. after his name. A Knight Grand Cross of an Order has the right to supporters to his arms and has a greater dignity and honour.

The Most Eminent Order of the Indian Empire

Instituted in 1877 when Queen Victoria was proclaimed

Empress of India. It has three classes: Knights Grand Commanders, Knights Commanders and Companions. The letters of distinction are G.C.I.E., K.C.I.E., C.I.E., respectively. This order also is in disuse.

The Royal Victorian Order

Instituted in 1896. This has five classes, namely, Knights and Dames Grand Class (G.C.V.O.); Knights and Dames Commanders (K.C.V.O., and D.C.V.O.); Commanders (C.V.O.); and Members (M.V.O.), there being a fourth and fifth class of this last.

This Order is awarded for services to the royal family.

The Most Excellent Order of the British Empire

This Order instituted in 1917 has five classes, as follows:
Knights and Dames Grand Cross: G.B.E.
Knights Commander and Dames Commander: K.B.E. and D.B.E.
Commanders: C.B.E.
Officers: O.B.E. and Members: M.B.E.
There is a further distinction within each class, into military and civil.

Owing to the unreasonable depreciation of the Order of Knights Bachelor, a movement arose among some Knights to establish a society to protect their rights. This came in 1908 with the foundation of the Imperial Society of Knights Bachelor (the Imperial of the title came from George V in 1912) and much has been done to elevate the status of Knights Bachelor and to give it greater position *vis-à-vis* the other Orders of knighthood. A special badge for Knights Bachelor was approved by George V in 1926.

Knights of St. John of Jerusalem

The full title of this Order is: The Grand Priory in the British Realm of the Venerable Order of St. John of Jerusalem. It represents a British revival of the old medieval Order of St. John of Jerusalem, which was founded in the Crusades in the eleventh-twelfth century. This latter still exists in Europe and throughout the world, and has a widespread charitable organization, as well as being highly developed in many other ways. When England followed the Protestant Reformation, the property of the Order in England went to the Crown, as did that of other monastic bodies. There ceased to be an English language branch or priory of the Order. But in 1888 it was incorporated in England, and in 1926 was granted the title of Venerable.

There are several classes in the Order but none of the decorations confer the title of Sir or Lady. The Order comes under the jurisdiction of the British sovereign and a prince of the royal house is always Grand Prior, which makes it curious that the knighthoods of the Order do not carry the normal titles. Even more is this the case, when it is realized that to become a Knight of Justice in the Order it is necessary to have a proven pedigree of several generations and to have arms borne by four great-grand-parents.

The classes of the Order with their abbreviations are:
Bailiff, or Dame, Grand Cross: G.C.St.J.
Knight of Justice: K.J.St.J.
Dame of Justice: D.J.St.J.
Knight of Grace: K.G.St.J.
Dame of Grace: D.G.St.J.
Commander: C.St.J.

Officer: O.St.J.
Serving Brother: S.B.St.J.
Serving Sister: S.S.St.J.
Associate: Assoc. St.J.
Chaplain: Chap.St.J.

None of these distinctions confer any title before the name of the owner.

Military Religious Orders

As the Order of St. John has been mentioned above as a relic of the old crusading days, it may not be out of place to refer to some other survivals. In the period of the Crusades, from 1095 to 1284 there were a number of Orders which had for their objective the warfare with the infidels or Moslems and the reconquest of the Holy Land. The most prominent of these were the Orders of St. John, of the Temple, and of the Teutonic Knights, also several Portuguese Orders. The Order of The Temple was dissolved early in the fourteenth century. The Portuguese Orders still exist, though they now have no longer any military significance. The Teutonic Order still exists in Germany.

The Knight of Glin

No one need be ashamed at being puzzled by this title, for the bearer of it is correctly referred to as Mr. Desmond J. V. FitzGerald, 29th Knight of Glin, so that the whole set-up is extremely hard to understand. As so frequently occurs in such matters, the subject cannot be understood without an historical explanation. The FitzGeralds are an ancient family in England, and still more so in Ireland which became their principal habitat. John Fitz-Thomas

FitzGerald, Lord of Decies, and Desmond, who was descended from the same family as the present Duke of Leinster, was a representative of the English Crown in Ireland in the thirteenth century, and as such claimed to be able to create his sons knights. Such power was often exercised by royal vicegerents in times past and indeed is still so exercised with the Queen's permission and licence when, for example, a civil servant in Fiji is created a knight, and is not likely to return home for some time. In such a case the Governor of Fiji will be empowered to confer the accolade. This would not explain the origin of the title of Knight of Glin, and indeed there is considerable confusion on the subject. According to some of the old writers on dignities, such as Betham and Russell, the three sons of the Lord of Decies were created knights by Edward III at the battle of Halidon Hill, 19 July, 1333. However, the fact remains that the descendants of these three knights have been styled as knights (but without the prefix of Sir) in Acts of Parliament, in patents under the Great Seal, and in all legal proceedings up to the present time. The three were: The Knight of Glin, already mentioned; the Knight of Kerry, and the White Knight. The last named, who is irresistibly reminiscent of Alice in Wonderland, was of a line now extinct. The Knight of Kerry is a baronet, so that he is of course styled Sir.

In fact these Irish knighthoods are hereditary knighthoods but without the title of Sir, the latter being just a curious Irish contradiction thrown in with this strange title for good measure. Perhaps the real explanation of the title is that in medieval times there would be small chance for any of the fighting FitzGeralds to obtain the accolade from a king of England, and so the title was conferred in perpetuity but when they became involved, as they did, in treasonable activities in the sixteenth century, the usage of the actual title of Sir naturally lapsed.

Mode of Address for newly created Knight

This does not differ from the usage with regard to peers, i.e. a man who has been named as a knight cannot be addressed as Sir until he has received the accolade, just as a new peer cannot be Lord until his title has been gazetted.

Knight's Widow

There is no change here because there is no hereditary title, and hence no dowagers. To avoid confusion between two knights' widows, or a widow of one knight and the wife of another, it is usual to print the name as follows: Lady (Joan) Smith.

NOTE.—In the event of the son of a viscount or baron, or the younger son of an earl being created a knight, his style is: The Hon. Sir James Smith, K.C.V.O., etc. His wife is then The Hon. Lady Smith (cf. the usage for a baronet's children, p. 40).

5 | Esquires, Gentlemen and Misters

ANYONE who troubles to look at the table of precedence which is printed in various books of reference will find that the last two entries are respectively for Esquires and Gentlemen. This must be mightily puzzling to those who have grown up in the modern usage by which everyone who receives a communication from a mail order house or a sales circular is styled Esquire. Yet it is only within the present century that this widespread usage of Esquire has occurred.

In Victorian times Esquire was jealously reserved for certain classes of people notably the landed gentry who were not otherwise titled, and was not given to city business men who had substantial fortunes and big and imposing city residences. The latter class were termed Mr. I have known in my experience at Burke's that if an addressing clerk should use the title of Mr. before the name of a squire the latter would indignantly return the envelope and complain that he had not been given his just rank. Actually today it seems to me more of a distinction to be called Mr. than Esquire since the latter must be shared with everyone whom the sellers of soap, book clubs, or football pools may wish to approach.

Yet seriously, Esquire was and still is offically a title

of honour and considerable kudos attached to its correct use. After the war when I was preparing the first post-war edition of *Burke's Peerage* I came to some old notes which belonged to the tables of precedence. Some of the notes on the subject of Esquire seemed a little overgrown and I requested the assistance of the College of Arms. One of the officers did indeed give me valuable assistance but he also assured me after grave deliberation that he did not think that doctors could be classed as Esquires but that lawyers could. As we shall see the entry of barristers into the privileged class of Esquires has hardly been allowed to pass without comment after more than 200 years.

The rules governing the use of Esquire after a person's name can be set out as follows: Those entitled to the use are:

1. The sons of all peers and lords of parliament during the lives of their fathers; the younger sons of peers after the deaths of their fathers; the eldest sons of the younger sons of peers and their eldest sons in perpetual possession.

2. Noblemen, of other nations, Minor Barons (Laird Barons) of the Baronage of Scotland.

3. The eldest (and probably all) sons of baronets and the eldest sons of knights.

4. Persons to whom arms are granted with the title of Esquire.

5. Esquires of the Bath and the eldest sons of those Esquires pursuant to the statutes of the Order.

6. Barristers-at-law by their office or profession.

7. Justices of the Peace, and Mayors while in commission, or in office (in Scotland this applies to Provosts only of Royal Burghs).

8. Persons attending on the Sovereign's coronation in some notable capacity or office of trust, or serving in some better class of post in the royal households.

9. Persons such as sheriffs of counties described as such in the Sovereign's commissions, or officers of the fighting services described as such in their commissions.

10. Attorneys in colonies, where the departments of counsel and attorney are united.

In addition to these classes there were two obsolete classes[1] which I will mention because they illustrate what was the old usage with regard to Esquire. These were: (1) Esquires created expressly with a collar of SS and spurs of silver[1] and (2) Persons who were chosen Esquires to the Body of the Prince.

In his origin, Esquire was an attendant on the person of a knight, and had to follow him in war. The Squire bore his knight's shield, looked after his armour and his wants generally and had to be possessed of many qualifications and accomplishments. He received in return some privileges and eventually looked forward to the degree of knighthood. This usage was of course in medieval times but the term Esquire came gradually to mean the first degree in gentry. From the rules set out above which have remained almost unaltered for 300 to 400 years, the term Esquire would thus come to mean most persons of any claim to gentility and position who were not otherwise titled.

It would be a mistake to regard an Esquire as one who had the right to a coat of arms, in other words an armiger, because instances occur in old days of people who were

---

[1] However, as late as about 1870, Queen Victoria created John Brown an Esquire.

styled Esquires being granted coats of arms. Nor again ought it to be taken that the term gentleman is synonymous with the possession of a coat of arms. Gentlemen were (and officially are) the rank below the Esquires and the lowest rank of gentility. This usage has long broken down if only for the widespread use of the word gentleman. Everyone is styled a gentleman today, and this habit may have sprung from the usage of solicitors who were wont to style their clients gentlemen when writing their wills.

It is quite out of the question to attempt to revert to the older usage of Esquire in these days of mass mailings and circularizations, but it may be of interest to note how important Esquire was as a title not much more than 250 years ago. One of the heralds of the College of Arms then made a note to inform the Earl Marshal (The Duke of Norfolk) of certain abuses. The third abuse was that lawyers assume coats (i.e. of arms) at their pleasure and the title of Esquire not being due to them. In the margin is the name of Sergeant Hendon who was apparently one of the offenders. This note was written in the reign of Charles II (1660–1685). So members of the Bar who are proudly, and as they deem of right, styled Esquires, may care to reflect that the usage is only a usage and that they might in theory be declared by the Earl Marshal to have no right to the title.

Mister, the full spelling of which Mr. is the abbreviation, is of course the medieval Master and as such was obviously used to describe persons of worship and honour. In the Middle Ages instances occur in which Master was used before the names of knights. It is perhaps fairly representative of the foreign *monsieur*, or *messer*. It is difficult to see why a term implying some degree of rule should be objected against by those wishing to claim superiority over others, but perhaps Esquire brought with it a connotation of landed rank and therefore of real estate.

Whatever the cause the title of honour in England has been, and evidently still is, Esquire, and with the adoption of this usage for the vast majority of people, Mister will become more than ever a rarity until at length someone discovers this fact, whereupon to possess it will be a distinction. It is in this way that a titled usage starts, and assumes great proportions.

It ought to be remembered that all usages of title, whether Mr., Esquire, or Lord or His Grace, are usages only; hardly one is a usage laid down by law, and therefore Mr. is as much a title as Lord. Curiously enough the full form of Mr. is found only in addressing a boy, Master John. An envelope is addressed, Master John Smith.

In the list of those entitled to the use of Esquire, mention was made of lairds in Scotland. This certainly needs a word of explanation. In Scotland the barons are understood not only as in England as the lowest rank in the peerage. There are lords of parliament and minor barons who are none the less dignitaries. These minor barons are the lairds, who really correspond to the squires, a race fast disappearing because of taxation. But a Scottish laird is usually one whose forebears owned the land for many generations before him. He will be referred to, not as John Grant, Esq., but as John Grant of Rothiemurchus. He is in fact not correctly referred to as Esquire which is an English usage and not applicable to him. His correct designation in writing is as shown above: John Grant of

Rothiemurchus, his full name followed, without any comma (this is most important), by the name of his estate. It is a simple usage one would think but there are great numbers of people who cannot grasp it. It is based on the old feudal usage whereby a man was known by the name of his estate. In Scotland in the country districts to this day this usage prevails and a man is known as Rothiemurchus, or Dalchully, or Morphie, or a peer may be called simply Rosebery. There is no disrespect in this but a recognition of the facts of property and a respect for landed worth.

As a general observation it may perhaps be said that the levelling up on titles as shown by the wide use of Esquire may be not a bad thing if it has any influence on people in making them more conscious of social values. Different classes have been refined in British history as qualities and possessions formerly thought beyond their reach have been brought downwards in the scale.

6 | Women's Titles

IT HAS generally been pointed out in the earlier chapters of this book that women's titles and precedence derive from men. This applies to their surnames. Whenever a woman is found who is very much incensed on the subject of women taking the surnames of their husbands, it is pertinent to ask what woman's surname she can find to take. Her own maiden name is the surname of her father, and even if a jealous Pankhurstism has induced her to use her mother's name, it is of course still the surname of a man, that of her own grandfather. The real objection to taking the husband's surname is that it is a relic of the time, not long past, when a woman became the property of her husband upon marriage. Still we must face the fact that a woman's title is derived from a man; if not from her husband then from her father.

There is an important exception to this principle: the position of a woman who is created a peeress in her own right. Her title derives from the Crown, and not from husband or wife. The peeresses now created under the Life Peerage Act, 1958, are an example.

The common usage as everyone knows, in Britain is for a single woman to be called Miss, and a married woman Mrs. The latter is an abbreviation or contraction for Mistress, the female equivalent of Master. Just as every man of worship or honour who had no other title was termed Mr., so his wife was Mistress. These titles of Mrs. and Miss are the product of centuries of social evolution and have no other basis.

With regard to the official scale of precedence, it is men's rank which confers precedence and regulates state ceremonials. At Court it is the husband's rank which is regarded, except in the case of peeresses in their own right.

With reference to the wife of an Esquire she is of course styled Mrs. like the wife of a Mr. The wives of peers, of baronets, and of knights are styled as shown under the chapters dealing with those dignities. There are still, however, many points about the styles of women which need attention.

There are many persons who hold high official positions which give them rank and precedence but which confer no rank on their wives. The outstanding example of this is the Archbishop of Canterbury who stands in the order of precedence at the head of all subjects and next to the princes of the blood, but whose wife not only has no precedence but is styled plainly Mrs. Fisher. This applies to the wives of all Archbishops and Bishops, and to the wives of most persons who hold high rank and precedence due to their official position.

A lady who is the daughter of a peer or baronet or knight retains her rank and precedence though married to a commoner.

The most vexed position of all is that of the titled woman who marries for the second time. The remarks which follow are equally applicable to this second marriage whether it follows on death or divorce, but they have the greater force today because of the large number of second or even third marriages due to the prevalence of divorce. There can be no argument that a woman who became Lady X by her first marriage and who married Mr. Smith, is not thereafter Lady X but Mrs. Smith. Nothing, however, is commoner than to find a woman who is the second or third wife of a peer using her title to which she is entitled in company with a first or possibly a first and second wife of the same peer. These previous wives have been divorced by or have divorced the peer and have married again. Why then do they not use their correct title, which is the name of the next husband? It seems a most extraordinary thing that there should be three Lady Mercuries all in the lifetime of the same man to whom they have been married. Are they all so enamoured of the title that even after they have discarded the man to whom it belongs of right, they still keep it?

Whatever the explanation for this strange phenomenon it does exist and is the cause of much confusion and also much altercation between newspapers and readers. Some newspapers with commendable courage refuse to use any but the correct title for a woman who has married again. Mrs. Brown of Tooting becomes Mrs. Smith of Wandsworth. Very well, so does Lady Apollo become Mrs. Snooks if her second husband has no other title. As for the usage, Constance, Lady Apollo, Mrs. Snooks, what on earth can be the justification for such a practice?

There remains the genuine case in which a peeress in her own right when she marries, retains her own rank and style, unless she has married a peer of higher rank than her own. Otherwise she is known as the Countess of Tooting, Mrs. Henry Stubbs (see pages 35–36).

Maids of Honour are given the prefix Hon. before their names and have the same rank as the daughters of barons. Formal mode of address would be: "Madam."

The Title of Dame

This title occurs in the Royal Victorian or British Empire Orders. The rule is that a lady so honoured has the title Dame prefixed to her Christian names, and the letters—G.C.V.O., D.C.V.O., or G.B.E. or D.B.E.—after her surname.

If a Dame is married to a peer, baronet or knight, she retains her married title with the appropriate letters after her name.

D.C.V.O. equals Dame commander of the Royal Victorian Order.

D.B.E. equals Dame Commander of the Order of the British Empire.

G.C.V.O. equals Dame Grand Cross of the Royal Victorian Order.

G.B.E. equals Dame Grand Cross of the Order of the British Empire.

An interesting rider on the subject of peeresses in their own right is that they do not confer any precedence or title on their husbands; for example the husband of one of the new life peeresses does not become a peer.

7 | Ecclesiastical Titles

W HEN we deal with ecclesiastical titles we come to a realm where long usage has sanctioned the style in many cases, but where none the less curious changes have taken place in recent years.

Any change in the past century would be recent in a sphere of such antiquity as that of church titles. The oldest titles have a history far antedating those of most secular styles. The chief of course is that of the Pope. The style "Pope" is not so much used in documents of a formal as of an informal nature. The ordinary signature of formal documents is Johannes P.P. XXIII. That is Johannes pastor pastorum XXIII. Pastor of pastors is a title which dates back some 1,200 years. Other titles which are in use for the Pope in official writings are: Johannes (or whatever is the name of the reigning pontiff) episcopus ecclesiae catholicae: Bishop of the universal church. Episcopus, servus servorum Dei. The Bishop, servant of the servants of God. Pontifex (Pontiff), Pontifex Maximus (Chief Pontiff, a title borrowed ultimately from that of the Emperors of pagan Rome who were the high priests of their polytheistic cult). Summus Pontifex. Romanus Pontifex. Sanctissimus. This last is the Most Holy which is applied to the Pope. Sanctissimus Pater. Most Holy

Father. Sanctissimus dominus noster. Our Most Holy
Lord. Sanctissima Sua. His Holiness. Beatissimus Pater.
Most blessed father. The usual style of address in writing
as in description is: H.H. Pope Johannes XXIII. *Begin:*
"Your Holiness" or "Most Holy Father", and end: "I have
the honour or profound veneration to be, Your Holiness's
most obedient servant [or child]." *Spoken address:* "Your
Holiness" or "Most Holy Father".

The next ecclesiastical degree below that of the Pope
is that of the Cardinals. They can be either bishops,
priests or deacons. In all cases their style as Cardinals is
in writing: To His Eminence Cardinal X. *Begin:* "My
Lord Cardinal" or "My Lord". *Conclude:* "I remain, My
Lord, Your Eminence's most devoted and obedient servant
[or child]." *Spoken address:* is: "Your Eminence."

If the Cardinal in question is, as often happens, an
Archbishop, his style is: His Eminence Cardinal X, Archbishop of Westminster, or H.E. the Cardinal Archbishop
of Westminster. As the red hat of a Cardinal is frequently
bestowed on ecclesiastics of the highest rank, it will often
occur that a Cardinal also holds an Archbishopric.

Apostolic Delegate. He is sent to represent the Pope
in a country—much like an Ambassador. Letters *begin:*
To the Most Rev. William Godfrey, Apostolic Delegate.
Begin: "Your Grace."

When we come to the other ecclesiastical ranks we deal
with those which are common to both the Roman Catholic
and Anglican Churches. These are the degrees of archbishops, bishops, deans, archdeacons, canons, priests and
deacons. There are three major Orders in the historic
Christian Church: bishops, priests and deacons. The rest

of the titles are purely historical growths which are refinements upon the three major Orders, but which can be very puzzling to a stranger to matters clerical.

Archbishop of Canterbury. *Letters:* To His Grace the Lord Archbishop of Canterbury. *Begin:* "My Lord Archbishop." *Conclude:* "I have the honour to be, My Lord Archbishop, Your Grace's most devoted and obedient servant." *Spoken address:* "Your Grace."

The full description of an Archbishop is: The Most Rev. Geoffrey Fisher. In the case of the Archbishops of Canterbury and York, the full style is: The Most Rev. and Rt. Hon. Geoffrey Fisher, P.C., D.D., etc. The reason for this is that the holders of the two Archbishoprics are also sworn of the Privy Council. Their offices are regarded as of such consequence that they should be able to give counsel in the Great Council of the kingdom. Similarly the Bishop of London who holds the most important see next to the two Archbishoprics is always a P.C. In many books in former generations the form has been reversed to show Rt. Hon. before Most Rev. or Right Rev., but this is incorrect and the proper form is as shown above.

Retired Archbishop. He is addressed as The Most Rev. Archbishop (Smith), etc. Here may be noted a curious fact applicable to all the episcopacy. It is a terrible solecism to refer to an Archbishop or Bishop *when he is in office* as Archbishop Fisher, or Bishop Wand. But once he has left office he is properly referred to as Archbishop Lang, or Bishop Cary. It may also be noticed that the use of the term Dr. for Doctor is quite usual when referring to bishops in office. Thus Dr. Fisher is perfectly correct as a description of the Archbishop of Canterbury both in speech and in writing. The use of

Dr. as applied to the episcopate is a fiction since at one time most of them had taken doctorates of Oxford or Cambridge, but now very few hold these distinctions of either of those universities or any other university. The tradition of learning persists as one of the attributes of episcopacy, though in most cases the doctorate if it exists at all is conferred *honoris causa,* by a university, or by the Archbishop of Canterbury as one of the Lambeth degrees.

Colonial Archbishops are referred to as: The Most Rev. the Archbishop of ———. *Begin letters:* "Most Rev. Sir." *Conclude:* "I have the honour to remain, Most Rev. Sir, your obedient servant."

Additional Notes:

In ceremonial documents the Archbishop is addressed as The Most Rev. Father in God, Geoffrey, by Divine Providence Lord Archibishop of Canterbury. He is Primate of All England.

Similar usage prevails with the Archbishop of York. He is Primate of England.

Bishops. *Letters:* To the Rt. Rev. the Lord Bishop of Birmingham.

Begin: "My Lord." *Conclude:* "I have the honour to be, My Lord, Your Lordship's obedient servant." *Spoken address:* "My Lord" or "Your Lordship."

The above usage applies to Bishops of the Anglican church who are diocesan bishops.

Bishops of the Roman Catholic Church are similarly styled, but should not really have the title Lord Bishop in England, where there is an established Church.

By courtesy it also applies to Bishops Suffragan and to Colonial or Missionary Bishops (though really Diocesan

Bishops alone should be styled Lord Bishop). Bishops of the Episcopal Church of Ireland, Scotland and Wales, where the Episcopal Church is no longer established, are styled in the same way as English Bishops, except that the Bishop of Meath and the Primus of Scotland are styled the Most Rev. (The Archbishop of Armagh is the Primate of All Ireland, the Bishop of Meath is the Premier Bishop of Ireland.) The Primus of Scotland is that Bishop who is the senior Scottish Bishop.

Retired Bishops. They are addressed as The Right Rev. Bishop Smith.

Begin: "Right Rev. Sir". An Archbishop of a colonial diocese receives preferment to an English bishopric, for example Archbishop of Brisbane became Bishop of London. Not until after his retirement is he known as Archbishop Ward.

Dean. Letters *begin*: To the Very Rev. the Dean of Manchester.

Begin: "Very Rev. Sir". *Conclude:* "I have the honour to be, Very Rev. Sir, your obedient servant." *Spoken address:* "Sir", and "Mr. Dean". In informal writing they are addressed as: "Dear Mr. Dean" and conclude, "Yours truly". There are fifteen Provosts of Cathedral Churches in England, i.e. parish churches which have lately had cathedral status, and they are addressed in the same way as Deans except that they are styled Mr. Provost, etc.

Archdeacon. Letters *begin:* To the Venerable the Archdeacon of Hampstead. *Begin:* "Venerable Sir."

Conclude: "I have the honour to be, Venerable Sir, Your very obedient servant." *Spoken address:* "Sir" or "Mr. Archdeacon".

Retired Deans, Provosts and Archdeacons are styled as with retired Bishops, the Very Rev. Dean X.

Canon. This can be taken in with the style of the ordinary clerk-in-Holy Orders, as The Rev. Canon Smith, etc. It bestows no special style.

Clerk in Holy Orders. Letters: To the Rev. John Smith. *Begin:* "Rev. Sir." *Conclude:* "I am, Rev. Sir, your obedient servant." *Spoken address:* "Sir."

It should be noted that the secular rank of a clergyman will make his clerical style vary, for example, if a clerk in holy orders is a peer, he will be: The Rev. the Rt. Hon. Lord X, and his address will vary to accommodate his rank as a peer.

With the exception of the higher ranks, the formal mode of address given above will seldom be used. Most Anglican parish priests would be surprised if their letters began as other than Dear Sir, or if the writer knew them slightly, as Dear Mr. —— A usage has grown up in the last fifty years of addressing the Anglican clergy as "Father". This has no validity whatever. Nor has it any more validity in the R.C. Church as far as the secular clergy are concerned. The distinction is between religious and secular. The religious in Rome are the monks who have taken the three vows of celibacy, poverty and obedience. In the Anglican Communion there are also many monks today. It is the religious or monks alone who can be called Father. Father Huddleston, C.R., of the Community of the Resurrection Mirfield, is an example in point. It has been said that the usage of Father as applied to the parochial Roman clergy is an invention of the last century due to misguided Anglican influence and that previously they were addressed as Mr.

clergy in the Anglican sense. Formerly the ministers of the Free Church denominations were known simply as Mr., just as their places of religious worship were termed not churches but chapels. Now the whole position has altered, for every chapel has become a church, and every minister is styled the Rev. just as if he were of the Established Church. This leads to great confusion because it is impossible to know from the style of The Rev. X whether a man is R.C., Anglican or Baptist.

The usage now followed in addressing Nonconformist Ministers is to prefix Rev. before their names, and *begin* their letters: "Sir". *Concluding with*: "I am Sir, yours faithfully."

Monks

The head of a monastery is an Abbot and his formal mode of address is either My Lord Abbot, Right Rev. Abbot of Nashdom or Right Rev. Father. It should be remembered that before the Reformation the mitred abbots of the greater monasteries in England sat in the House of Lords and that in the first part of the reign of Henry VIII before his quarrel with Rome, there was a majority of spiritual lords in the Upper House. The greater abbots yielded place only to the episcopate in precedence. Formal letters *conclude*: "I beg to remain, My Lord Abbott, your obedient servant."

The head of a province of an order of monks, for example, of the Dominicans, referred to as The Provincial is addressed as Father Aloysius, while the *written address* is: "Very Rev. Father." *Conclude:* "I beg to remain, Very Rev. Father, your obedient servant [or child]." The address on the envelope is To the Very Rev. Father etc.

Before leaving the subject of ministerial modes of address it may be as well to add that monks of the various orders have letters following their names, thus S.J. means Society of Jesus, the proper title of the Jesuits. O.P. means Ordo Predicatorum, or Order of Preachers, i.e. the Dominicans. In the Anglican Church many religious orders now exist, the product of the Oxford Movement and the Anglo-Catholic Movement over the past 100 years. Consequently we find Anglican Dominicans and Franciscans, as well as specifically Anglican orders such as the Society of the Sacred Mission at Kelham, abbreviated S.S.M., and the Community of the Resurrection, Mirfield, C.R. Some Anglican monks use the term Dom before their names, for example, Dom Gregory Dix. This term is short for Dominus; it may be added that no comment is offered by the present writer on the appropriateness of the various clerical titles, or their agreement with the Gospel spirit.

Women also figure among the lists of ecclesiastical titles. Not that there have been female bishops, except for one case in America, pre-war, when a lady bishop appeared as chief pastor for an organization known as the Pillar of Fire. But women have for many centuries rivalled men in the austerities of religion, and orders of religious life for women exist in great profusion. The matter of title is not difficult to deal with. The head of a nunnery is the Mother Superior, the Rev. Mother. The nuns who have taken the threefold vows are known as Sisters, and are usually addressed as Sister Mary or Sister Angela, often by a name which they take on entering religion, as it is called.

.   .   .   .   .

Alexandria, of all Egypt, of Nubia, Ethiopia, the Pentapolis, and all the country evangelized by St. Mark.

The Ethiopian Church: His Beatitude The Abuna of Ethiopia (or Abyssinia).

In general therefore the heads of the various branches of the Eastern Orthodox Church are styled His Holiness or His Beatitude.

Styles of address are therefore: *Patriarch.* His Holiness The Patriarch of ——. *Begin:* "Your Holiness." *Conclude:* "I have the Honour to be, Your Holiness's obedient servant." *Metropolitan:* His Beatitude The Metropolitan of ——. *Begin:* "Your Grace." *Conclude:* "I am, Your Grace's obedient servant."

The title of Pope was at one time generally applied to all heads of patriarchal sees, Rome being one of them. Gradually in the West the title was restricted to the Pope of Rome, since there were no other sees of equal importance in the west. But in the East the term Pope came to be applied to all the parish priests; after all it only means "father".

Outside the Christian orbit altogether comes the title of the leader of British Jewry, the Chief Rabbi, the Very Rev. Israel Brodie. The mode of address to the Chief Rabbi is: The Very Rev. The Chief Rabbi, or The Very Rev. Dr. Israel Brodie.

The Jewish Rabbis are addressed as The Rev. Rabbi J. Smith. The opening and conclusion of a letter, if formal, are the same as for the clergy of Christian denominations. Should the Rabbi be, as often happens, a Doctor of some faculty in a university, his style is merely altered to The Rev. Rabbi Dr. J. Smith.

8 | Military, Naval and Air Force Titles

BEFORE going into the subject of service titles, it would be useful to have a clear view of the relative ranks in the three services:

AIR FORCE	NAVY	ARMY
Marshal of the Royal Air Force	Admiral of the Fleet	Field-Marshal
Air Chief Marshal	Admiral	General
Air Marshal	Vice-Admiral	Lieutenant-General
Air Vice-Marshal	Rear Admiral	Major-General
Air Commodore	Commodore 1st and 2nd Class	Brigadier
Group Captain	Captain	Colonel
Wing Commander	Commander	Lieut.-Colonel
Squadron Leader	Lieut.-Commander	Major
Flight Lieutenant	Lieutenant	Captain
Flying Officer	Sub-Lieutenant	Lieutenant
Pilot Officer	Acting Sub-Lieutenant	2nd Lieutenant
No equivalent	Warrant Officer— —Midshipman (formerly)	Conductor Royal Army Ordnance Corps, Master Gunner, 1st Class, 1st Class Staff-Sergeant-Major

AIR FORCE	NAVY	ARMY
Warrant Officer	No equivalent	All Warrant Officers Class 1 except those marked above
Warrant Officer 2nd class	No equivalent	Warrant Officer, Class II
Flight Sergeant	Chief Petty Officer	Squadron Quartermaster Corporal or Squadron, Battery, Troop, or Company Quartermaster - Sergeant, Colour - Sergeant, Staff Corporal or Staff Sergeant
Sergeant	Petty Officer	Corporal of Horse (Household Cavalry) or Sergeant
Corporal	Leading Seaman	Corporal; Bombardier
No equivalent	—	Lance-Corporal
Leading Aircraftman=L.A.C. Aircraftman, 1st class=A.C.1. Aircraftman 2nd class=A.C.2.	Able-Seaman; Ordinary Seaman	Trooper, Gunner, Sapper, Signalman Driver, Guardsman, Rifleman, Fusilier or Private

The rule may be simply stated : with regard to the commissioned ranks given above they are all addressed by their ranks prefixed before their names, except in the case of Sub-Lieutenant in the Navy, 2nd Lieutenant in the Army, and Pilot Officer in the Air Force. The last named are addressed as : John Smith, Esq. This is the rule as given in the guide-books but it is completely out of order as regards the Air Force, where an officer's rank is, in my experience, always given, even in the case of Pilot Officers. Moreover, in courses of instruction for officers, they are or were during the war at least instructed to give their rank, even at the lowest, at the head of their papers and letters. Whether the rule still applies in the Navy and Army I cannot say, though I know that it formerly did.

In the case of officers of the three services who are titled, their service ranks of course take precedence of their civil rank, so that Air Marshal Sir Dermot Boyle, or Admiral Earl Mountbatten are the usual forms, while the full form would be Admiral the Rt. Hon. the Earl Mountbatten. In general usage the peerage title would tend to drop out and only the service title be used.

Each of the three services has women's services attached to it. In the Women's Royal Air Force, there is first a Commandant-in-Chief, who is Her Majesty Queen Elizabeth the Queen Mother. Then next in rank comes the Air Chief Commandant, H.R.H. the Duchess of Gloucester. The ranks of the W.R.A.C. then begin and run as follows:

Air Commandant	Squadron Officers
(usually a D.B.E.)	Flight Officers
Group Officers	Flying Officers
Wing Officers	Pilot Officers

All these ladies are addressed as "Ma'am" by those in lower ranks.

In addition there is attached to the Air Force, the Princess Mary's Royal Air Force Nursing Service.

The Air Chief Commandant is H.R.H. Princess Royal.

The Air Commandant is usually a D.B.E. Below her are the following ranks: Group Officers, Wing Officers, Squadron Officers, Flight Officers, and Flying Officers.

The Navy has the Women's Royal Naval Service. The ranks there are The Director, who is a Commandant, Superintendent, C/O, i.e. Chief Officer, and then First, Second, and Third Officer. Here again address is "Ma'am".

The Women's Royal Army Corps has as Commandant-in-Chief, Her Majesty the Queen Mother. The Controller Commandant is H.R.H. Princess Royal. After these come in descending order of rank, Brigadier, Colonel, Lieut.-Colonel, Major, Captain, Lieut., 2nd Lieut.—just as in the male service.

Before passing on from Air Force ranks, it may be noted that the apparent ranks given to the airmen, or rankers, are not ranks at all, but trade qualifications. The L.A.C., the A.C.1, and the A.C.2, are the trade classifications associated with the rank which in the Air Force is equivalent to private in the Army. Most emphatically an L.A.C. does not correspond to a Lance-Cpl., though he is often given work to do which in the Army would be given to a very junior N.C.O. It is a curious fact that in the American Army the private is followed by a private first class, a classification which depends on behaviour and skill, and is almost a rank jealously guarded by those who attain it.

There are many curious anomalies in service ranks, which have sprung up over the course of centuries. A Lieut.-General ranks higher than a Major-General, which seems curious until we realize that a Major-General was originally Sergeant-Major General and so the subordinate rank.

In foreign armies there is a strong resemblance in the rank structure and it is not hard to obtain charts of relative rank, though in peace-time few people are likely to wish to have this information.

There is one delightful fact about military ranks. However exalted an officer's rank, he can always be addressed as "Sir" and this is sufficient distinction.

Modes of address: The formal style is: "Sir": *conclude:* "I have the honour to be, your obedient servant." Admirals, Vice-Admirals, and Rear Admirals are addressed as Admiral: Generals, Lieut-Generals, and Major-Generals as General. Chaplains are addressed as other clergymen, except that the Chaplain of the Fleet, the Chaplain-General etc., is given this style on his envelopes or letters; other chaplains may have C.F. added to their names. In the R.A.F. again, a difference may occur, for example, Squadron Leader the Rev. ——.

9 | Personages of the Law

THE principal legal dignitary in Britain is the Lord Chancellor. His style is: The Rt. Hon. the Lord High Chancellor (of Great Britain). Otherwise he is addressed as for a peer, a rank which he always holds, sometimes as a life peer, but usually as an hereditary peer.

The Lord Chancellor is the head of the legal profession, but this was not always indisputably the case. The Lords Chief Justices of the Exchequer and of the Common Pleas would certainly have regarded themselves as equals at least with the Lord Chancellor. But since the Judicature Acts of 1873 and subsequently, the position of the Chancellor as head of the whole legal profession has been quite clear. His appointment is a political one, and he is one of the three law officers of the Crown. The other two are: the Attorney-General and the Solicitor-General. Both of these, like the Chancellor, are members of the Bar, despite the title of Solicitor-General borne by the last named.

The Attorney-General is addressed in letters: To the Rt. Hon. Sir (John) Smith, Attorney-General, Q.C. Beyond this his mode of address is as for a baronet.

The Solicitor-General is addressed as for the Attorney-General. Both he and the Attorney-General are knighted on appointment.

The Lord Chief Justice is the chief as his name implies of the Judges. Formerly there were two Lord Chief Justices, one of the court of the Exchequer and the other of the Common Pleas; these courts were the original in which royal justice was dispensed. But in addition to these royal courts there was the court of the monarch's secretary or Lord Chancellor. When a suitor of the royal courts found that for some reason or another (possibly because there was no recognized mode of action) he could not proceed with his suit in those courts he often approached the Lord Chancellor's Court, and made his petition there. Hence the jurisdiction of the Lord Chancellor whose court arose originally because he was the keeper of the sovereign's conscience, and had to see that equity was done, or if not why not. For centuries this curious dual system persisted in English law, and it was not until 1876 that law and equity, as the two systems were called, were merged and after that time, only one office of Lord Chief Justice remained.

The Lord Chief Justice is addressed in letters: The Rt. Hon. the Lord Chief Justice of England, or The Rt. Hon. Lord Smith, Lord Chief Justice of England. The latter form would be correct now, for the Lord Chief Justice is nowadays created a peer, although there were celebrated Chief Justices of the eighteenth century who were not higher in rank than knights. For the rest the Lord Chief Justice is addressed as in the case of a Judge of the High Court, see below.

The Lord Justice of Appeal who sits in the Appeal Court is addressed as The Rt. Hon. Lord Justice Holborn, or The Rt. Hon. Sir Edward Smith, as for a Judge, see below.

Judges of the High Court are also termed Puisne Judges. The latter term comes from an Old French corruption of Latin, i.e. post (Latin, after), nè, born; thus meaning junior in rank. In *written address* they are: To the Hon. Mr. Justice Jones. Letters *begin*, "Sir"; and *end*: "I have the honour to be, Sir, your most obedient and humble servant." The *spoken address* is: "Sir" or "Sir Norman" or whatever the Christian name may be. But this does not apply when they are on the judicial bench. They are then styled: "My Lord" or "Your Lordship".

Judges of the County Courts of England and Wales. *Written address* is: To His Honour Judge Smith. *Spoken address* is (on the Bench): "Your Honour". The title His Honour is retained after retirement. This title of Judge Smith or whatever the name, is a curious instance of the only case in which a judicial personage is styled as Judge. A Judge of the High Court is, as seen above, never styled Judge (though in conversation outside court, a barrister is correct in addressing a High Court Judge as "Judge" but this is a usage peculiar to the Bar).

Justice of the Peace. By far the greatest number of courts in England and Wales are presided over by Justices of the Peace who are unpaid. These are the familiar J.P.s who perform so many of the necessary functions of dispensing justice. They are addressed on the Bench as: "Your Worship" and in very formal letters as The Rt. Worshipful John Smith, J.P., but apart from this have no official title, though they are of course entitled to have the letters J.P. after their names. Stipendiary magistrates are always barristers.

Deputy-Lieutenant and Lord-Lieutenant. While dealing with the matter of J.P.s it may be as well to clear the position of the D.L. This is Deputy-Lieutenant, and is often held by a J.P. He is as the name implies a Deputy of the Lord Lieutenant. The latter is usually but not always a nobleman. He is addressed as: H.M. Lieutenant of Blankshire, and then follows his rank, the Rt. Hon. the Earl of —— or Sir Thomas Smith, Bt.

The High Sheriff is a ceremonial rank which carries little or no duty with it today but is a relic of the days when the Sheriff was the principal administrative officer of a county. The High Sheriff is always a man of substance but is more often than not untitled.

Official Referees of the Supreme Court (England and Wales). They are addressed as: To His Honour Sir Tom Eastham, or His Hon. Brett Cloutman, according to name and ranks. Letters *begin*: "Sir."

Master of the Rolls. This Judge is in charge of the Public Record Office. He is usually a peer. He is addressed in writing: To the Rt. Hon. the Master of the Rolls, or To the Rt. Hon. Lord Evershed, and so on according to rank. Letters *begin* and *conclude* as those to a Judge. *Spoken address* is "Sir", but not when on the Bench, where it is "My Lord" or "Your Lordship".

Vice-Chancellor. His letters and spoken address are as for a Judge.

The Scottish Legal System
This of course is quite separate from that of England,

it being one of the provisions of the Treaty of Union, 1707, that Scottish legal system and procedure should remain independent. The Scots law is in any case based on Roman Law, which has influenced English Law but does not form its basis.

The Lord Advocate for Scotland. This is a political appointment. He is styled, in letters: To the Rt. Hon. the Lord Advocate. Letters *begin*: "Sir." He is not necessarily knighted, and after his retirement from the post, he does not keep the prefix Rt. Hon., unless he is a Privy Counsellor. Thus the style would normally be Rt. Hon. John Mackenzie, Q.C., M.P. (while he is in office).

Solicitor-General for Scotland. There is no formal style, nor is the holder of this political appointment necessarily knighted. The holder, for example, is styled simply, William Robertson, Esq., Q.C., M.P.

Lords of Session. These are the Judges of the Court of Session corresponding to the Judges of the High Court in England. There are fourteen Judges who are Lords of Session. Two of them bear additional titles, the first as Lord President and Lord Justice General, and the second Lord Justice Clerk.

The Lord President and Justice General, corresponding somewhat to the Lord Chief Justice, is styled: (in writing), The Rt. Hon. Lord Justice General. *Begin:* "My Lord." *Conclude:* "I have the honour, My Lord", etc., as for a peer. The same style is used for the Lord Justice Clerk.

The Lords of Session are styled: The Hon. Lord Cochrane, etc. This title of Lord is retained for life, even after retirement. His wife is called Lady and her letters begin: "Madam", as in the case of the wife of a baron. She is personally addressed as "Your Ladyship". Letters to a Lord of Session begin: "My Lord", etc., as in the case of a Baron. The prefix Hon. is used unless the Lord of Session is also a Privy Counsellor when he is termed Rt. Hon. The retention of the honour of the title of Lord for life is covered by an Order in Council of February, 1905.

Dominion Judges. The title of Hon. is borne by the following:

Chief Justices and Judges of the High Court of Australia.

Chief Justices and Judges of the Supreme Courts of New South Wales, Victoria, Queensland, South Australia, Western Australia, Tasmania, New Zealand, and South Africa.

Chief Justice and Judges of the Supreme and Exchequer Courts of Canada.

Chief Justice and Judges of certain other Courts in the Provinces of Canada.

Some of the above are permitted to retain the title after retirement.

Letters *begin*: To the Hon. John Smith, or to: The Hon. Mr. Justice Smith.

Judges of Colonies are styled His Honour while in office.

Serjeants-at-Law. This rank has disappeared as none have been created for a generation. When it occurs in books, etc., the style was Serjeant or Mr. Serjeant Sullivan otherwise as Esquire.

Writer to the Signet is entitled to the letters W.S. after his name.

Queen's Counsel is entitled to Q.C. after his name but both he and W.S. are otherwise addressed as Esquires.

10 | Governors, Ambassadors and Diplomats

GOVERNORS-GENERAL exist in the various British Dominions which no longer include areas such as Pakistan, formerly part of the British Empire in India and which after it obtained independence was for a time a British Dominion under a Governor-General, but has now become a republic, which like India, is within the Commonwealth. Canada, Australia, New Zealand and South Africa are the territories which possess Governor-Generals. The style used is (in writing): To His Excellency Governor-General Sir Edward Smith or the Rt. Hon. Lord Clarendon. Of the four territories just mentioned two at present have Governors-General who are native-born, those for Canada and South Africa, so that the complication of the style of a Governor-General by a peerage or other title is unlikely to exist.

Governors of Colonies are addressed in writing: To His Excellency Governor Sir Edward Jones or To His Excellency Sir Edward Jones, Governor of Jamaica, or again To His Excellency John Smith, Esq., Governor and Commander-in-Chief of British Honduras. Letters *begin*: "Sir." *Conclude:* "I have the honour to be Your Excellency's faithful and obedient servant." *Spoken address:* "Your Excellency."

Wives of Governors-General. The official style is Her Excellency. Since 1924 (June) this official style has been confined to these ladies, whereas previously all wives of Governors of Provinces, Colonies, etc., as well had been addressed as Her Excellency during the period of the husband's tenure of office. This last usage was purely of courtesy. It is probable that it is still used unofficially in colonies and territories of like nature.

Lieutenant-Governor. is generally called His Honour This again is a usage of courtesy, not formal arrangement.

A Governor does not retain his title of His Excellency after his term of office is over.

Members of Colonial Executive or Legislative Council have the prefix Hon. before their names, thus: The Hon. John Smith.

Ambassadors

British Ambassadors are addressed in writing: To His Excellency Her Britannic Majesty's Ambassador Extraordinary and Plenipotentiary to the Republic of France. Letters *begin*: "Sir", or according to the Ambassador's rank. *Conclude:* "I have the honour to be, Sir [or My Lord, if his rank is that of a peer] Your Excellency's most humble and obedient servant." He is addressed in speech as "Your Excellency". Wives of Ambassadors have no official title but from courtesy are styled Her Excellency when they live in the capital to which the husband is accredited. This style should not be used in England.

Foreign Ambassadors in Britain. They are addressed in letters as: His Excellency the Ambassador Extraordinary and Plenipotentiary of the Republic of France. Otherwise they are styled exactly as British Ambassadors. The wife of a foreign Ambassador to the Court of St. James is styled (for courtesy) Her Excellency.

Envoy Extraordinary and Minister Plenipotentiary. He is addressed in accordance with his rank as Her Britannic Majesty's Envoy Extraordinary and Minister Plenipotentiary.

Minister Resident is addressed in letters as: To John Smith, Esq., Her Britannic Majesty's Minister Resident to the Republic of Liberia. *Begin:* "Sir." *Conclude:* "I am, Sir, Your Most obedient servant." *Spoken address:* is "Sir".

Consul, Vice-Consul, Consul-General and Agent and Consul-General as case requires. He is addressed: John Smith, Esq., H.B.M. Consul, etc.

Immunity of Ambassadors and their staffs. In theory an Ambassador as representing a state on business and coming under flag of truce has always been regarded as possessing personal immunity among civilized peoples but there have been many cases in the history of great nations, for example in the times of Greece and Rome, when such immunity was violated. In modern times better codes of behaviour have prevailed. Some credit for this must go to the stand taken in Britain, laid down under an Act of Parliament of Queen Anne, 1708. This Act was called "for preserving the privileges of Ambassadors and other publick Ministers of Foreign Princes and States ". It was occasioned by an assault on the person of the Russian Ambassador and his detention for some hours. Under this Act not only Ambassadors but also their servants and entourage, if duly registered with the Principal Secretary of State, possess diplomatic immunity and cannot be sued in the British courts.

11 | Heralds, the College of Arms and and Lyon Office

ALTHOUGH no official styles are used for addressing the English Heralds, it may not be out of place to deal with their official titles as these can occasion great difficulty until one is familiar with them.

For the past 400 years there have been thirteen Officers of Arms at the College of Arms in Queen Victoria Street. These are the Officers known to the general public as the Heralds, just as the College of Arms is popularly known as Herald's College, although it is not so called by its own Officers, but is styled by them the College of Arms.

The College is under the rule of the Earl Marshal, who is the Duke of Norfolk. His office is hereditary and he is styled His Grace, etc., just as any other Duke. The Earl Marshal is one of the great Officers of State, and the Officers under his jurisdiction are part of the Sovereign's household. In the Middle Ages every great nobleman had his heralds who looked after matters affecting coats of arms, precedence and the like. The King had more heralds than anyone else, and in 1484 they were formed in England into a College or fraternity in order the better to administer matters of arms.

The thirteen officers are: Three Kings-of-Arms. They are Garter, Clarenceux and Norroy. Garter is so named because he was from early times associated with the Order of the Garter founded in 1348. Clarenceux was named from the Duke of Clarence of Plantagenet times. Norroy was an abbreviation or contraction of Nord Roi or North King, because he had, and still has, jurisdiction over arms and pedigrees north of the Trent. Then there are six Heralds, namely Chester, Lancaster, Richmond, Somerset, Windsor, and York. These are mostly named from the titles of Plantagenet Princes, the children of Edward III. After these come four Pursuivants or junior Heralds (the word Pursuivant means follower), who are the most junior officers of the College. They are: Bluemantle, Portcullis, Rouge Croix, and Rouge Dragon. These names come mainly from various badges or emblems in use in the royal house in Plantagenet times.

These Officers are all addressed in accordance with their respective rank. Thus the Kings-of-Arms are usually knights, so created after their appointment, and the Garter King-of-Arms will accordingly be addressed as: The Hon. Sir George Bellew, K.C.V.O., Garter King-of-Arms. In this case he happens to be the younger son of a peer, Lord Bellew, and so has the prefix "Hon". The holder could however be the ubiquitous John Smith, Esq., in which case he would be addressed as such, with Garter King-of-Arms following his name. The remaining Officers of the College are addressed in the corresponding manner, suited to their rank in ordinary life, whether they are peers, knights or esquires, and followed in each instance by the name of their respective office.

In Scotland the position is somewhat different in so far as the Lord Lyon who is the person responsible in Scotland for matters of arms is the equivalent of the Earl

Marshal and not of one of the Kings-of-Arms. The Lord Lyon is a great Officer of State in Scotland, and when a separate Scottish government existed, he held the rank and place of a Privy Counsellor. The appointment of the first holder of the office is unknown but a Lord Lyon was knighted in 1318 and the holder is always so honoured.

The style of the Lord Lyon is: The Rt. Hon. Sir Thomas Innes of Learney, K.C.V.O., Lord Lyon King-of-Arms. If the present holder were not a Knight he would still be termed Rt. Hon.; this has nothing to do with his personal rank but with his tenure of office of Lyon. With reference to the designation "of Learney" this is the description of a Scottish laird (see under chapter on Esquires and Gentlemen), by which the territorial designation is tacked on to the name and no comma comes between. If Sir Thomas were not a knight, he would be correctly addressed as Thomas Innes of Learney, without Mr. or Esquire, and he would be correctly referred to as Learney.

Lord Lyon is a judge of the Court of Session, as Lyon Court is part of the judicial system of Scotland.

The Scottish Heralds are Albany Herald, Marchmount Herald.

Pursuivants—Kintyre, Unicorn, Carrick.

In addition there are also Pursuivants Extraordinary—these being Linlithgow and Falkland. These latter officers are appointed to carry out certain duties which are required by Lyon.

Heralds Extraordinary. These are appointed (in England) from time to time, in recognition of heraldic knowledge and attainment, and because some urgent ceremonial is at hand, such as the Queen's Coronation when three were appointed. These three (attached to the English College of Arms) were Norfolk and Arundel Heralds Extraordinary and Fitzalan Pursuivant Extraordinary.

Chief Herald of Ireland. Until 1940 the Ulster King-of-Arms held sway over matters heraldic over the whole of Ireland. The holder of the office who had seen the great change from British to Irish Free State Government, died in that year. After this the Irish Government wished to have the office of Ulster withdrawn from Ireland and to meet their wishes it was so done, and united with that of Norroy King-of-Arms in the College of Arms. The north of Ireland comes under the sway of the Norroy and Ulster King of Arms. In the Irish Republic, a new official was appointed, who was a civil servant, and who was given the office of Chief Herald of Ireland. This title follows his name, for example, Gerald Slevin, Esq., Chief Herald, etc., and his address is the same as that of his predecessor in Dublin Castle.

12 | Civic Dignitaries

LORD MAYOR. While there are many Mayors, there are comparatively few Lord Mayors. In England there are seventeen, namely: London, York, Liverpool, Manchester, Birmingham, Leeds, Sheffield, Bristol, Newcastle-upon-Tyne, Bradford, Norwich, Hull, Leicester, Nottingham, Portsmouth, Stoke-on-Trent, and Plymouth. In Wales, there is Cardiff, and in Ireland, Dublin, Belfast and Cork.

The Lord Mayors of London, York, Belfast, Dublin, Sydney, Melbourne, Adelaide, Perth, Brisbane and Hobart only have the right to be addressed as Right Hon. Letters are addressed: To the Rt. Hon. the Lord Mayor of London, or To the Rt. Hon. Sir William Smith, Lord Mayor of London. The prefix Rt. Hon. is not taken into retirement. The rest of the style is the same as for a baron. The wife of a Lord Mayor is styled Lady Mayoress, she is personally addressed as "Your Ladyship", and her letters *begin*, "Madam", during the time of her husband's tenure of office.

In the case of other Lord Mayors letters are addressed: To the Rt. Worshipful the Lord Mayor of Bristol.

Mayor (of a city) is addressed as: The Right Worshipful the Mayor of Burton and letters *begin*, "Sir". *Conclude:*

"I am, Your Worship's most obedient servant." *Spoken address:* "Sir" or "Madam". The Mayor of a Borough is styled: The Worshipful the Mayor of Croydon, and letters *begin*, "Sir".

Lord Provost. This is the equivalent of the Lord Mayor in Scottish corporations. The Provost is the equivalent of Mayor.

The provosts of six Scottish cities, namely Edinburgh, Aberdeen, Glasgow, Dundee, Elgin and Perth are styled Lord Provost, but only the Lord Provosts of Edinburgh and Glasgow are entitled to Rt. Hon. before their names. These two are therefore addressed as: The Rt. Hon. the Lord Provost of Edinburgh, etc., or The Rt. Hon John Crawford, Lord Provost of Edinburgh. The rest is as for a baron, but the title is not retained after retirement either for Lord Provost or Provost. Lord Provosts of other cities are addressed as: The Lord Provost of ——, etc. There is no special status for wives of provosts in consideration of their husband's offices.

Chairman of the London County Council. Letters *begin:* To the Rt. Hon. the Chairman of the London County Council or To the Rt. Hon. Herbert Smith, Chairman of London County Council. *Begin:* "Sir", and *conclude:* "I am, Sir, yours faithfully," etc.

Trinity House, The Elder Brethren of. This is the Corporation of Thames Pilots founded or incorporated by Henry VIII. The Elder Brethren are addressed as Captain.

13 | British Government

PRIME MINISTER. He is addressed according to rank, thus The Rt. Hon. John Smith, M.P., Prime Minister and First Lord of the Treasury. In previous times when peers were often Prime Ministers, they would have been addressed according to their rank but no peer is now ever selected as Premier.

Cabinet Ministers. They are addressed as Rt. Hon. before their names.

Ministers not in the Cabinet are also addressed as the Rt. Hon. but not Junior Ministers unless they are Privy Counsellors. In fact the use of Rt. Hon. is given to Ministers because they are Privy Counsellors and not because of ministerial status. Rt. Hon. is used before the name but the words P.C. are not in that case given after the name.

Privy Counsellors. Letters *begin*: To the Rt. Hon. John Smith, unless the P.C. is a Duke or Marquess when the appropriate opening for his rank is used. The letters begin and end according to his rank. P.C. is not used after the name when the style Rt. Hon. is prefixed before it.

Privy Council of Canada. Members are styled the Hon.

Secretary of State. Letters *begin*: To Her Majesty's Principal Secretary of State for the Home Department, or, To the Rt. Hon. the Earl of Cassilis (or whatever may be his rank), Her Majesty's Principal Secretary of State for the Home Department. Otherwise the style is as for the particular rank.

Member of Parliament. He is addressed according to rank, since he may be of military or naval or air force rank, or a baronet or knight. He cannot be a peer with one exception but a son of a peer who bears a courtesy title can be a Member of the Commons. The exception is in the case of Irish peers who have never been elected to sit in the House of Lords. They can be elected to a seat in the Commons and thus we had for forty-seven years The Rt. Hon. the Earl Winterton, M.P. M.P.s are entitled to have the letters M.P. after their names.

High Commissioners of the Dominions in London were entitled to the prefix Hon., unless they had higher rank, as when they are P.C.s. Cabinet Ministers in British Dominions (except Canada), are styled Rt. Hon. if they are P.C.s, otherwise the Hon. This applies to Australia and New Zealand, not to South Africa, where no prefix is used. In Canada, Hon. is used if the Minister is also a P.C.

High Commissioners are now ranked with Ambassadors and except in the case of Southern Rhodesia they are addressed as His Excellency, the High Commissioner for

Canada. *End:* "I have the honour to be, Sir, Your Excellency's most humble servant." In speech the address is: "Your Excellency."

Additional note on Honourable as title in Dominions.
This is borne for life by all members of the Canadian Privy Council and of the Executive Councils of Australia and of the states of Victoria and Tasmania. Also in the Executive Councils of the various Dominions and among Ministers of three years tenure of office and various senatorial presidents, the title of Hon. is retained on retirement.

14 | Miscellaneous

Probably there is more difficulty with titles which arise through change of social habits. For an example, there is the usage which has grown up over the past twenty-five years of describing someone as emeritus. This word was correctly used for a retired professor, and he was referred to as Professor Emeritus Smith. The usage was varied so that he appeared as the Emeritus Professor Smith. This was a legitimate usage in academic circles and it was useful to distinguish a professor who had retired but who still lived on in the University or College and to distinguish him from those who held appointments. However, the word emeritus has spread in meaning to take in all manner of occupations so that cases occur of Organist Emeritus, and even Verger Emeritus. This is bordering on the ridiculous and it has acquired a very stupid meaning when it is given to people such as a retired vicar, or even a bishop. This sort of thing is really a piece of jargon, and should be discouraged as much as possible.

Academic titles are the cause of much confusion, and in titles I include degrees. None of those who hold academic appointments are entitled to special modes of address other than those required by polite behaviour. What is perhaps more important to those who have to use directories and to address people who are in the higher ranks of the teaching profession, is to know how to place the various degrees and appointments. One of the most ludicrous manifestations of vanity is in the use of large numbers of letters after a person's name. I once remember when dictating to a secretary, using the letters after a man's name, Sir Thomas Smith, R.S.V.P., C.O.D., L.R.C.P., etc. All of this rigmarole was taken down in good faith by the girl, and reproduced on an envelope. I then showed her the mistake, but it was an example of the mesmeric effect which letters after a man's name do have upon other people who do not understand how they are obtained.

There are large numbers of fellowships of societies, which can be obtained on the payment of a subscription, and which are open to anyone who is recommended by two members of the society. In one case I received a letter from a learned society asking me to become a member. Had I have done so, I should have been entitled to call myself a fellow of that society. My knowledge of the particular subject of that body was very limited, but there I should have been as a fellow of the society. Now it is only necessary to have three or four of these and immediately people are impressed. So much is this the case that I knew one instance where a man wanted to obtain some furniture on H.P. terms and had to give a personal reference. He asked his general manager to give him one. The manager who used a number of letters after his name, gave the reference on office note-paper. So impressed was the furniture supplier that he did not bother with any further references but considered that one was enough from a man who had thirteen or fourteen initials after his name. The real status of some of these letters can easily be gauged. The really outstanding fellowships are the F.R.S. and the F.B.A. Fellow of the Royal Society implies an eminence in scientific work which would be outstanding anywhere in the world. Fellow of the British Academy implies a cultural attainment on a level with the position of the scientist in the Royal Society.

Then there are a number of fellowships which are not obtainable merely on the payment of a subscription. These fellowships are carefully distinguished from membership in the particular society. Everyone who is eligible is elected to membership, but in several societies a fellowship can only be given when a number of years has passed or when the member in question has reached some position of eminence in the particular profession.

When letters are placed after a person's name and when he has many of them it is advisable to pick out those which are important. In the case of a scientist if he is an F.R.S. that is probably sufficient although one can add D.Sc., or Sc.D. (Doctor of Science) according to the style adopted in various universities for abbreviating a Doctorate of Science. But to give all the degrees and fellowships possessed by such a distinguished scientist as Lord Adrian is just to render the subject slightly absurd.

A man who has reached Adrian's position will probably hold a dozen honorary doctorates. One of these, and probably several, will be the LL.D., The LL.D. is the stand-by of the academic world and is given to anyone who is to be honoured by a University and cannot well be given a D.D., a D.Litt., or doctorate of any other faculty.

The selection of the important letters varies with the man. A journalist who has to write to an inconsiderable country magnate, had better give him not only his J.P., but his F.S.A. if he possesses it. On the other hand, to put F.S.A. after the name of a man who has the O.M. is decidedly to gild the lily. Anyone who is eminent enough to become an O.M. needs no lesser mark of distinction after his name.

The writer, particularly the journalist, ought to be on his guard against the stupefying effect of a collection of letters of the alphabet. But there is no doubt that the general public will go on with an almost superstitious reverence for the various abbreviations which are to be found in the lists at the beginning of *Who's Who* and *Burke's Peerage*.

There are a number of titles which will gradually become rarer but which are still capable of causing a lot of difficulty. These titles are from the East. Many of them come from the former Indian Empire and were native titles which were adopted by the British administration when it governed India. These titles can be very puzzling and as there are still many holders of them and as literature contains numerous references to them, I think that it would be a good idea to give a few notes about them.

In the former Indian Empire there were orders of rank as follows: Among the Hindus there are the following gradations in rank: 1, Maharaja Bahadur (Bahadur meant warrior and it was bestowed as a mark of distinction); 2, Maharaja; 3, Raja Bahadur; 4, Raja; 5, Rai Bahadur; 6, Rai Saheb; 7, Rai. Among the Moslems the following was the order: 1, Nazim (the only holder of this in India was and is His Exalted Highness the Nizam of Hyderabad); 2, Nawab Bahadur; 3, Nawah; 4, Khan Bahadur; 5, Khan Saheb; 6, Khan.

These words have come into English from various Indian, Turkish and other oriental languages because of our association with India.

There is the term Amir which is perhaps more familiar in English as Emir. The Amir was the sovereign of Afghanistan. He is now usually called the King of Afghanistan. Emir is a term applied to various tribal chiefs especially in Africa. But Amir or Emir means a Moslem chief.

The Babu was the term given to the clerical class in India. They were very junior civil servants, and the word has a meaning somewhat similar to Mister.

Khan was the ruler of a small Moslem state but in the usage under the British Empire in India it meant only an honorific title. The Maharaja was a Hindu title and meant great prince. The feminine of it is Maharani. Mir is another title similar to Khan. Nawab was a title given to some of the rulers under the old Mogul government which preceded the British Empire in India. The Begum is the feminine of Nawab. The term Raj meaning king or Kingdom was taken over by the British, and their government in India was the British Raj.

Saheb or Sahib was simply a native term applied to a European, and meant roughly master. Saheb was used of course only for a white man, but there were a few other Indian and oriental terms which hung on under the British connection as applied by the British to some of their Indian officials.

Thus the Risaldar was the commander of a troop of

horsemen, and was a native officer of cavalry in the Bengal and later the Indian Army. The Subadar was another native officer in the army. It also meant the governor of a province. The Zemindar was a Moslem tax-collector. Sirdar is a corruption from Sardar and meant an exalted official. Under British suzerainty Egypt had a British officer as Sirdar of the combined Anglo-Egyptian forces. The late Earl Kitchener was perhaps the most eminent of the Sirdars. The word Sultan has a similar meaning to the word Sirdar and was applied very widely throughout the Orient to rulers of independent states.

Then there are some terms very much in use, at least until a few years ago, in Egypt and North Africa. There was the title of Bey, and that of Pasha. A Pasha was a person of high rank in the Turkish armed forces or in government service. The Pasha went on in Egypt after the Turkish connection was ended. Now in Egypt there are no more Pashas and the title has been abolished. Effendi is the equivalent of esquire or more properly mister, because in Egypt the European will usually be addressed as Effendi, where it can only mean sir, or mister.

Hajji is a person who has made a visit to Mecca and in other words has acquired a considerable merit by making this pilgrimage. There are many Hajjis in Moslem countries and sometimes they are distinguished by a mark or band on their headgear. The Kadi was a judge in the old Turkish court. The Mufti was a counsel in the old courts who used to give opinions when asked, on legal matters. The word Sheikh is perhaps one of those most familiar to English readers owing to the very strange idealization of the rulers of Arab tribes which has been a feature in the West for some time. The word Sheikh means literally an old man and it is applied to most rulers of Arab tribes.

The word Dey is fairly familiar because of its application to the rulers of Algiers and of Tunis. Then there is the Khedive who was the ruler of Egypt. Both the Dey and the Khedive were representatives of the old Turkish Empire which in theory stretched from Turkey in Asia Minor to the Atlantic and Morocco. As time went on the various rulers made themselves independent of the Sultan of Turkey and so the Khedive of Egypt was practically free from interference by the Sultan. This was a strange position and had curious results. It so happened that in 1914 Egypt was in some sense formerly a part of the Turkish Empire. To settle the matter once and for all Britain established a protectorate over Egypt, and from this, after the First World War, came the Kingdom of Egypt. The Kings of Egypt are descended from the Khedive.

These notes about various foreign or oriental titles may be useful in clearing up the arguments and interests which come to light through reading.

When we turn to foreign titles in England we usually mean titles used on the continent of Europe. Indeed it does not require much thought to realize that a foreign title must be a European title in its origin. Europe colonized North and South America, Australia, and the greater part of Africa. Consequently the titles of Count or Baron which are found in Latin America and elsewhere outside Europe are titles of European origin.

The subject of European titles is one of the most difficult and its difficulties have been increased in our time. To begin with, the only books which gave information on this subject have long since ceased to be published.

One book was the Marquis de Ruvigny's *Titled Nobility of Europe*. This book was produced in 1914 and endeavoured to give a reference to every foreign title in Europe and in the United Kingdom. However, there are so many titles in Europe that even in 1914 when Ruvigny's book was produced it was impossible to give every title.

Then there was the very fine publication, the *Almanac de Gotha* which was published first in 1763 and which ceased in 1944. This was a tragedy because the book ceased not because it could not be produced or because people had lost interest but solely on account of the capture of the plates of the work in Silesia at the town of Gotha, by the Russians. Despite all attempts at producing a similar book to the *Gotha* no one has yet succeeded in doing so.

As a result, there are numerous instances of people who call themselves by a continental title whose credentials cannot be checked. There is no reference book where they can be looked up. If anyone calls himself a peer or baronet, then there are three or four books in which his name can be found. If the name is not found therein there are two explanations, or possibly three; he may have been newly created and not got his name in the latest edition. He may be the claimant to a title the succession to which has not been determined; or maybe an impostor. Many bogus counts and other alleged title holders are wandering about Europe and America.

There seems to be no way of checking these various titles except to have recourse to the Embassy of the title-holder's country. If the French Embassy knows nothing about a Count, then it may safely be said that his claims are suspect. The real nobility of France are fairly well known and are certainly known to the officials of the French Republic. In fact to some extent aristocracy is protected in France. A person is not allowed, as he is in England, just to take a famous French name. The Notary will not allow a change of name so that some refugee from central Europe should suddenly become a Bourbon, or Rohan. In England he of course can become Howard, Cromwell, Grosvenor. I wonder very much if he would be prevented from taking the name of Windsor.

As regards the arrangement of titles, as I have pointed out earlier in this book the British titles with the exception of Earl come from the continent of Europe. Duke is from the Latin Dux, Marquis is simply the ruler of a march, a meaning which is well brought out in the Italian form of the word, Marchesa. The titles in Germany are different and run as follows: Herzog (Duke); Furst and Reichsfurst (Prince); Graf (Count); and Barons. There are distinctions between the nobilities of the old Holy Roman Empire which became extinct in 1806, and the noble castes of the various German states which existed, up to 1918, as part of the German Empire under the headship of the Hohenzollerns.

There were likewise several systems of peerage in France, where indeed the word peer originated, but all titles of nobility were abolished at the period of the French Revolution in 1790. New systems of nobility came into existence after the restoration of the Bourbon monarchy, and again under the first empire (that of Napoleon I) and the second empire (that of Napoleon III). These distinctions do not, however, affect the usage of the titles, and duc, marquis, comte, vicomte and baron are in the order with which we are familiar in the British peerage.

In Spain there are distinctions between the haute noblesse and the nobleza titolada. The former have the Grandeéship and the latter do not. There are distinctions again between the grandees of the highest antiquity as confirmed by royal decree under the Emperor Charles V in 1520 and the other classes.

The names of the titles in Spain are duque, marques, conde, visconde, and barone. Portuguese titles follow the same line, as do those of Italy, in the latter case having the terms, Principe, Duce, Marchese, Conte, Visconte, Barone, Signore, Nobile, Patrizio, and Cavaliere. Some of the latter titles may be a little difficult to equate with English titles, but if we recall that Esquire and Gentlemen are still terms given in the List of Precedence we shall understand the Italian concept of Signore and Cavaliere.

It must be remembered that western Europe once formed a united realm as far as institutions were concerned; it was Christendom and had the same system in nobility as in other things. Therefore a Spaniard or an Italian, a German or a Portuguese can easily understand the systems of class and nobility which prevailed in his respective country and in neighbouring lands.

There are none the less certain distinctions between Continental and British systems. In Continental countries all members of a family are noble. In Britain only the peer himself and his wife are noble, even though the title is hereditary. There is no class in Europe which is really corresponding to the untitled aristocracy of Britain, the ancient landed gentry.

In Russia there are several variations from the norm of aristocratic title in the rest of Europe. The ancient class of boyars were the original nobles, and this class has received no additions since 1682. There were many regulations issued by the Tsars and these made five classes —the princes, counts, barons, untitled gentlemen of an antiquity before the reign of Peter I, and those of later date.

It may be observed that Prince is a far more frequent title in Europe than in England where it is confined to members of the reigning royal house. Archduke is again a title not known in this country but used in Austria and the term Grand Duke was used in Russia as applied to certain princes of the royal line.

The terms of H.R.H. and H.H. need explanation. H.R.H. is sometimes used for the head of a family but not for the rest of his line, who are simply H.H. There was a familiar example of this in the case of Princess Marie Louise, who although she was the granddaughter of Queen Victoria was simply H.H. Her father had been H.R.H. Prince Christian of Schleswig-Holstein but in this line while the head of the family was H.R.H., the rest were H.H. only.

H.E.H. is His Exalted Highness, and is used only of potentates such as H.E.H. the Nizam of Hyderabad, or of certain German princes of the old régime. His Serene Highness has a curious ancestry as a mode of address. It was used in the later Middle Ages by those who had to communicate with princes who were felt to be of a lesser rank than some of the great dignitaries, yet whom it was desired to honour. An example is that of the Prince of Monaco, the head of the ancient Grimaldi family. He is styled H.S.H. and this for reasons which go back some 400 or 500 years. The Serene or Most Serene was the title given to the Doge or Duke of Venice and who was reckoned a great prince but not quite on an equality with the King of France or Spain. It would be easy to go on for a long time dealing with the titles conferred at various times, or assumed by European monarchs.

The principle in dealing with Continental nobility is that the mode of address is fairly simple. A Continental nobleman can always be addressed as M. le Duc etc. This is perfectly respectful but avoids any difficulties which may be felt over mode of address. In one sense there is less formality than in England.

Those who wish to read more on the subject of foreign titles would do well to peruse an article on Continental Nobility written by Mr. Philip Thomas in the 1953 (Coronation) edition of *Burke's Peerage*. Also there is another work by the Marquis de Ruvigny namely *The Titled Nobilities of Europe* which was limited to some 250 copies but which is more useful in many ways than the author's larger *Titled Nobility of Europe* to which reference has been made above. This smaller work gives information in turn about each country's noble system.

Many people are puzzled by the title of the Aga Khan. A note on this may be of use, as the family are continually in the news. The position as I have been able to ascertain it from the Colonial Office is as follows:

"The grandfather of the late Aga Khan (the famous race-horse owner) was the first Aga Khan to establish relations with the British and in 1844 he was granted the title, His Highness, in recognition of his spiritual leadership of the Ismaili Khojas and for his life. (It should be stated that the Ismailis were not a landed and concentrated community but a sect of the Moslem religion and their head was not a territorial magnate but a kind of Pope, in virtue of his descent from the Prophet Mohamed.) After his death the title was again granted for life to his son and subsequently to the late Aga Khan on his succession to the Imamate (the title given to the spiritual rulers in Islam). It is not, therefore, an hereditary title and Her Majesty recently continued the title to the present Aga Khan again in recognition of his spiritual leadership of the Ismaili community and strictly for the duration of his life.

"The position with regard to the correct style of members of the Aga Khan's family does not appear to have been previously defined. The Aly Khan, for instance, is often referred to as Prince Aly Khan and has been so described in Government House Court Circulars issued from Government House, Bombay, in 1936–37, but the appellation had no basis in official orders and the Government of India acknowledged no authority for the use of the title Prince."

A class of nobility which can cause much concern at first sight is that of Malta. There are some thirty of them, with titles of Marquis, Baron, etc. In their own islands they are recognized as nobility, and by a concordat with the British Government their titles are clearly guaranteed. It is somewhat difficult for them with regard to their titles when they visit England, as they can hardly be styled as though they were British nobility, but if they use the foreign style, as M. le Marquis, they may be construed as being foreigners, which they are not.

In Canada there are a few cases of titles recognized by

the British Government when it took over the government of that country. There were Seigneurs in Canada and one Baron (De Longueuil) whose titles were granted by the French kings, and which were recognized by the British.

Index

THE RIGHT WAY TO SPEAK IN PUBLIC

A. G. MEARS, A.S.D., Gold Medallist, London Academy of Music

4th revised edition. ONE OF THE GREAT BOOKS OF ALL TIME. Are you nervous? Can you hold your audience? Clear step by step instruction. Essential for public speakers.

English Illustrated: . . . "Will teach confidence for public speaking in any language."

RELEASE YOUR VOICE AND FIND YOUR PERSONALITY

MARJORIE HELLIER

This is not an ordinary, dull elocution book but a gaily written and illustrated guide for those who wish to make the most of their voice and learn the art of good speaking. The author's teaching methods are widely famed and this book should help not only ordinary people but television, stage and film stars as well.

CONDUCT MEETINGS, CONFERENCES AND DISCUSSIONS

H. M. TAYLOR (Head of Abbey School for Speakers) and A. G. MEARS

4th revised edition. *The* standard work on the subject. For all Committee Members and those in executive positions.

The Head Teachers' Review: . . . "Terse . . . lucid . . . efficient . . . excellent." The most comprehensive and outstanding volume on the subject.

HOW TO WIN CONFERENCES, MEETINGS AND INTERVIEWS

W. D. ELLIS and F. SIEDEL

Vital to Chairmen, Secretaries, Treasurers, executives and politicians. Vital also to YOU because it explains the secrets of handling people. Indicates mistakes you've probably made in personal relationships. Emphasizes importance of presentation, method, timing. A MUST if you want to get ahead.

THE CONVERSATION SECRET

ELLIOT RUSSELL

This astounding book will help YOU. Covers: Breaking the ice — Small talk — Interest — Listening — What to talk about — Where thoughts arise — The thought drift — Finding topics — Choice from store-away mind — Collecting material — Exercises — Etiquette, etc.

Sheffield Telegraph: ". . . Packed with sense."

Western Evening Mail: . . . "The art of talk is in danger . . . we do not realise what we miss if unable to indulge freely . . . banish shyness in easy natural way." Unique in its simple, direct instruction.

7s. 6d. *each*

ELLIOT RIGHT WAY BOOKS
KINGSWOOD, SURREY

THE RIGHT WAY TO TAPE RECORD   LAURENCE MALLORY

EFFICIENT THINKING, REASONING AND CONVERSATION
         DR. T. A. RYDER, B.Sc.(HONS.) PH.D.

PSYCHOLOGY AND YOU
         DR. T. A. RYDER, B.Sc.(HONS.), PH.D.

BISHOP'S GARDENING ENCYCLOPEDIA
         B. W. BISHOP, F.R.H.S.

FETES AND BAZAARS FOR PROFIT
         S. HOMEWOOD and J. WHITE

HOME MEDICAL ENCYCLOPEDIA
         "DIOCLES", M.R.C.P., M.R.C.S.

THE RIGHT WAY TO KEEP PET FISH
         REGINALD DUTTA, B.A., F.Z.S.

THE RIGHT WAY TO KEEP DOGS
         R. C. G. HANCOCK, B.Sc., M.R.C.V.S.

KIT WILSON'S CAT ENCYCLOPEDIA   KIT WILSON

TECHNIQUE OF BRITISH SALESMANSHIP   A. G. ELLIOT

SEA FISHING AND TACKLE TINKERING   W. E. DAVIES

FRESHWATER FISHING AND TACKLE TINKERING
         W. E. DAVIES

MORE GOLF SECRETS   DR. H. A. MURRAY

WALTER'S HORSE KEEPERS' ENCYCLOPEDIA
         W. H. WALTER

THE RIGHT WAY TO SWIM   WINIFRED GIBSON

GUN FUN AND HINTS   A. G. ELLIOT

PAINTING IN OILS AND WATERCOLOUR   D. J. SMITH

CINE CAMERA SECRETS   LAURENCE MALLORY

RIGHT WAY TO PLAY CHESS   D. BRINE PRITCHARD

ALL ABOUT MEN   JOSEPH H. PECK, M.D.

7s. 6d. *each*

ELLIOT RIGHT WAY BOOKS
KINGSWOOD, SURREY